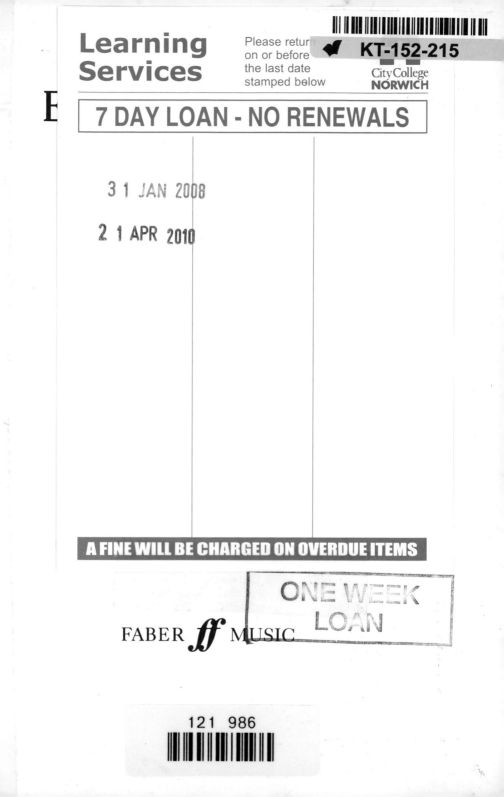

FABER *ff* MUSIC

© 1993 by Faber Music Ltd
First published in 1993 by Faber Music Ltd
3 Queen Square London WC1N 3AU
Cover design by Shirley Tucker
Printed in England by Halstan & Co Ltd
All rights reserved

ISBN 0 571 51328 X

PICTURE CREDITS

The author would like to thank the following institutions and individuals who have very kindly supplied pictures:

Royal College of Music: 2, 18, 19a, 19b, 22, 31, 33, 41b, 41c, 48, 52b, 92c, 98, 99, 101, 117a; Mary Evans Picture Library: 7b, 17c, 21, 41a, 68, 69, 74c, 75a, 82b, 83a, 88, 90, 94b, 103a; Steinway & Sons: 8b, 23a, 38a, 42b, 43a, 43b, 71, 74a, 74b, 75b, 75c, 103b; John Broadwood & Sons: 11, 14a, 76; Wendy Thompson Collection: 40, 42a, 57; Russell Collection, Edinburgh: 102; Decca Record Company: 5, 55 (Photo: Mary Robert); Harrison Parrott: 78, 122; Isolde Ohlbaum: 13b; Lies Askonas: 17b; Terry Harrison Artists: 32; Clive Barda: 34; EMI Classics/Iain McKell: 50; Brigitte Lacombe: 52a; Malcolm Crowthers (1992): 64; Sony Classical: 72; Victor Hochhauser: 86; Instituicao José Relvas, Alpiarça: 92a; Vivienne Purdon: 92b; Museen der Stadt Wien: 93; Christian Steiner: 115; Harding Museum, Chicago: 117b; Yamaha Corporation: 121

FOREWORD

This is a music dictionary with a difference. It is designed specially for aspiring pianists of all ages from 12 to adult. The definitions cover all the main terms, forms, styles and techniques likely to be encountered in keyboard music of all periods, together with concise descriptions of early and modern keyboard instruments. Alongside this are biographical sketches of famous pianists and composers of keyboard music, with an outline of their principal keyboard works.

I gratefully acknowledge the major contribution made by Wendy Thompson in the preparation of this dictionary and the selection of the illustrations.

Fanny Waterman
Leeds, June 1993

A

A (1) Note name. The A above middle C

vibrates 440 times a second,and is the pitch to which many musical instruments are tuned.

(2) **A major, A minor**. The name given to the major or minor scale beginning on the note A. Pieces of music based on these scales are in the key of A major/minor.

(3) A term used to describe the first section of a piece. A piece in ternary form (ABA) resembles a sandwich.

a *(It.)* In, to, at; **a tempo**, in time.

aber *(Ger.)* But.

accelerando, accel. *(It.)* Gradually getting quicker.

accent Stress, emphasis on a particular note. Written: > . The first beat in each bar will normally have a slight accent.

acciaccatura *(It.)* 'Crushed note'. A musical ornament in which another note is played a split second before the main note. Written:

accidental A sharp, flat or natural placed before a note to alter its pitch to one not in the key-signature of the piece.

accompaniment The name given to the secondary part of a piece of music where the other instrument or part carries the main tune or theme. In piano music, one hand can 'accompany' the other; in a violin sonata, for instance, the piano usually 'accompanies' the violin, although it can work the other way round when the main musical interest is in the piano part!

acoustics The science of sound.

action The name given to the workings of a piano, especially the rise and fall of the hammers.

adagietto *(It.)* Slightly faster than *adagio*.

adagio *(It.)* Slow.

'Adieux, Les' See **'Lebewohl, Das'**.

ad libitum Freely, taking one's own time.

affettuoso *(It.)* With feeling.

affrettando *(It.)* Hurrying.

agitato *(It.)* Agitatedly, hurriedly.

air A simple, melodic tune, possibly in the style of a folksong, e.g. *The Londonderry Air.*

Isaac Albéniz

Albert, Eugen d' (1864-1932) German composer and pianist. He was born in Glasgow and studied in London. His virtuoso technique won the admiration of Liszt. Made many international concert tours, but in later life turned to opera composition. He was briefly married to the virtuoso pianist Teresa Carreño. Piano works include a Concerto (1884), a Suite (1883), a Sonata (1893) and four books of piano pieces.

alcuna *(It.)* Some; **con alcuna licenza**, with a certain degree of freedom.

al, alla *(It.)* To; **al niente**, 'to nothingness', dying away; **al segno**, 'to the sign', i.e. find the sign 𝄋 marked above the score of a piece and play on from there; **alla tedesca**, in the style of a German dance.

Albéniz, Isaac (1860-1909) Spanish composer and pianist, a pupil of Liszt. Wrote over 200 piano pieces based on Spanish idioms, including a set of 12 pieces called *Ibéria* (published in 4 volumes between 1906 and 1909).

Alberti bass A characteristic figure made up of broken chord patterns and found in the left hand of some piano pieces; e.g. Mozart's Sonata in C, K545. Named after the Italian composer and harpsichord player Domenico Alberti (*c.*1710-1740), who used it a great deal.

Alberti bass

etc.

Albrechtsberger, Johann Georg (1736-1809) Austrian organist, composer and teacher, who worked at St Stephen's Cathedral in Vienna and at the Viennese court. His best-known pupil was Ludwig van Beethoven.

alborada *(Sp.)*   A dawn song. Ravel's *Alborada del gracioso*, from his piano suite *Miroirs* (1904-6), is a famous example.

Albumblatt *(Ger.)*   Album leaf. A short piano piece, the sort that might be written into a child's scrapbook or an adult's autograph album. Much used by 19th-century German composers such as Schumann.

Alexeev, Dmitri (b.1947)   Russian pianist. Studied at the Central Music School of the Moscow Conservatory. Won 2nd prize in the 1969 Marguerite Long Competition in Paris, 1st prize at the 1975 Leeds International Piano Competition. For 12 years after his Leeds success he was refused permission to play in the West, but since the late 1980s he has enjoyed a flourishing international career.

al fine *(It.)*   (Go) to the end.

Alkan (real name Charles Henri Valentin Morhange, 1813-1888)   French pianist, composer and teacher. He wrote a great deal of extremely difficult piano music, including many sets of variations on operatic airs and a set of 12 studies (all in minor keys), and died when a heavy bookcase fell on him.

alla *(It.)*   See **al**.

alla breve *(It.)*   In cases where the time-signature of a piece is 4/4, but the speed of the music is too fast for four beats in a bar, *alla breve* indicates that the basic beat-unit should be a minim, i.e. 2/2.

alla marcia *(It.)*   In the style of a march.

allargando *(It.)*   Broadening out and slowing, often getting slightly louder at the same time.

alla turca *(It.)*   In Turkish style. Mozart wrote several pieces in this fashionable 18th-century style, including the *Rondo alla turca* from the A major Piano Sonata K.331.

allegretto *(It.)*   At a moderate speed, less fast than *allegro*.

allegro *(It.)*   Fast and lively; **allegro moderato**, moderately fast; **allegro ma non troppo, allegro ma non tanto**, fast, but not too fast; **allegro commodo**. at a comfortably fast speed; **allegro con brio, allegro con spirito**, fast, with fire or spirit; **allegro sostenuto**, fast but sustained; **allegro assai, allegro vivace**, very fast indeed.

allemande *(Fr.)*   An old German dance-form, played at a moderate speed, much used by Baroque composers such as J.S. Bach. Earlier allemandes were often in duple time, but later ones tended to be written in quadruple metre, almost always with an upbeat. The allemande was often used as the opening movement of the Baroque suite. By the late 18th century, the dance-form had merged with the newer German Dance (Mozart's German Dances, K571, for piano, were originally published in Paris under the title 'Allemandes'.)

all'ottava *(It.,* often written **8va)** See **ottava**.

al segno *(It.)* 'To the sign'. See **al, alla**.

amoroso *(It.)* Lovingly.

anacrusis The unstressed up-beat(s) where a piece of music does not begin on the first beat of the bar.

ancora *(It.)* Still, yet: e.g. **ancora più presto**, even quicker.

andante *(It.)* At a moderate, flowing speed.

andantino *(It.)* A little quicker than *andante*.

animando *(It.)* Becoming more lively.

animato *(It.)* Lively, spirited, animated.

animez *(Fr.)* Get more lively.

a piacere *(It.)* See **piacere**.

appassionato *(It.)* Impassioned, in a passionate style. Beethoven's Piano Sonata no.23 in F minor, Op.57, is titled *Sonata appassionata*.

appoggiatura *(It.)* 'Leaned'. A musical ornament in which another note is played just before the main note, 'leaning' into it. Written:

arabesque *(Fr.)* A decorative, swirling musical style, very appropriate for piano music, derived from Moorish art and architecture. Debussy's *2 Arabesques* (1888) were his earliest published piano pieces.

Argerich, Martha (b.1941) Argentinian pianist, a pupil of Michelangeli. Won 1st prize in the 1965 Chopin International Piano Competition, and has since enjoyed a worldwide career.

arietta *(It.)* A little song.

aria *(It.)* A song (usually from an opera or oratorio), or a songlike piece.

arioso A piece in songlike style. The slow movement of Beethoven's Piano Sonata no.31 in A flat, Op.110, is marked *Arioso dolente* (in the style of a sad song).

Arne, Thomas (1710-1778) British composer of stage works, notable as the composer of *Rule, Britannia!*. Wrote 6 keyboard concertos and a book of harpsichord sonatas.

arpeggio   The notes of a chord played one after the other in succession.

Arrau, Claudio (1903-1991)   Chilean pianist. Studied in Berlin, winning several major international prizes. From 1935 until his death, he was internationally acclaimed for his poetic interpretation of the mainstream piano repertory. Settled in the USA, 1941.

Art of Fugue   One of J.S. Bach's very last works, exploring all the possibilities of fugal writing. Often played on the keyboard, although Bach specified no particular instrument.

Ashkenazy, Vladimir (b.1936)   Russian pianist, a pupil of Lev Oborin at the Moscow Conservatory. 2nd prizewinner in the 1955 International Chopin Competition, 1st prizewinner at Brussels in 1956. In 1962 he was a joint gold medallist (with John Ogdon) in the Tchaikovsky Competition in Moscow. He left Russia for the West the following year, and has since played all over the world. Now equally famous as a conductor.

Vladimir Ashkenazy

assai *(It.)*   Very; **allegro assai**, very quick.

assez *(Fr.)*   Quite, moderately; **assez vite**, fairly fast.

a tempo *(It.)*   In time, or resume the original speed.

attacca *(It.)*   Attack. Carry straight on from one section to the next without a break; **attacca subito**, attack instantly.

aubade *(Fr.)*   A morning song, the same as *alborada*.

augmented   Made larger, stretched. An augmented interval or chord is one made bigger by a semitone. The time-value of a note may also be augmented by adding a dot, which increases its length by half.

augmented 6ths   Various types of chromatic chords, which often act as pivotal points in a harmonic progression. They mostly occur on the minor 6th degree of the scale. There are 3 main types:
    French 6th, consisting of major 3rd, augmented 4th and augmented 6th above the bass note
    Italian 6th, consisting of major 3rd and augmented 6th above the bass note
    German 6th, consisting of major 3rd, perfect 5th and augmented 6th

above the bass note

augmented 6ths in the key of C major

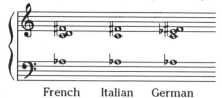

French   Italian   German

aural training   The training of a musician's ear, through recognition of intervals, accuracy of pitch and rhythm, etc.

ausdrucksvoll *(Ger.)*   With expression.

avant-garde *(Fr.)*   'The advance-guard'. A term given to composers (or their music) who pioneer experimental trends or styles, often rejecting former practices in the pursuit of the totally new.

B

C.P.E. Bach accompanying Frederick the Great

B (1) Note name. In German, B natural is called H and B flat is called B.

(2) **B major, B minor**. The name given to the major or minor scale starting on the note B, and also to the keys based on those scales.

baby grand The smallest size of grand piano.

Bach, Carl Philipp Emanuel (1714-1788) German composer, third son of J.S. Bach. He worked at the court of Frederick the Great of Prussia at Berlin, and then at Hamburg. One of the most important keyboard composers of his time, C.P.E. Bach wrote an influential treatise on keyboard playing, and over 200 sonatas and concertos.

Bach, Johann Christian (1735-1782) German composer, youngest son of J.S. Bach. Worked in Italy and London. Mainly noted for his operas, but also wrote nearly 40 piano concertos (which greatly influenced the young Mozart), and many piano sonatas.

Bach, Johann Sebastian (1685-1750) German composer, one of the greatest of the Baroque period. He worked as organist in several small Thuringian towns, and then at the courts of Weimar and Cöthen before being appointed Kantor at St Thomas's, Leipzig, where he remained until his death. Bach wrote a good deal of music for keyboard (harpsichord and organ), including 13 harpsichord concertos with string accompaniment; 16 concertos for solo harpsichord; 6 English and 6 French suites for harpsichord; the *Goldberg Variations* and the *Italian Concerto* for harpsichord (both included in the collection known as the *Klavierübung*); 15 2-part and 15 3-part inventions; 7 toccatas and fugues, and the two

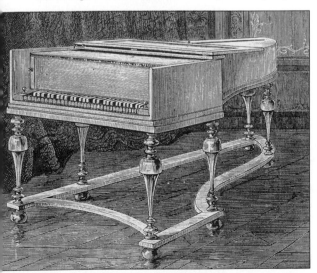

Silbermann piano of 1746, played by J.S. Bach

J.S. Bach: A page from the Clavierbüchlein vor Wilhelm Friedemann Bach, 1?

books each of 24 preludes and fugues called *Das Wohltemperierte Klavier* (*The Well-Tempered Clavier*, or 'The 48'), as well as collections of teaching pieces for his eldest son and his second wife Anna Magdalena. Organ works include 28 preludes and fugues; 6 sonatas; 4 toccatas and fugues; and many other fantasias, fugues, etc., together with numerous chorale preludes, including 46 in the *Orgelbüchlein* (Little organ book).

Bach, Wilhelm Friedemann (1710-1784)   The eldest son of J.S. Bach. A talented keyboard player, he was recognized as one of the best organists of his time; in later life he held no regular job, and died in poverty. He wrote many keyboard pieces, including concertos and sonatas.

Bachauer, Gina (1913-1976)   Greek pianist, a pupil of Cortot and Rakhmaninov. Won the 1933 International Piano Competition in Vienna, and then pursued a worldwide career, based in London.

Backhaus, Wilhelm (1884-1969) German pianist, one of the greatest of the 20th century. Studied at the Leipzig Conservatory, and then in Frankfurt, making his début in 1900. Won the 1905 Rubinstein Prize, and embarked on an international touring career, making important early recordings of the Chopin *Études* and the Beethoven concertos. One of the greatest Beethoven and Chopin interpreters of his generation,

Gina Bachauer

his repertoire embraced the German classics and the romantics. Reputed to be able to play any Bach prelude and fugue at will. His career spanned 70 years.

badinerie, badinage *(Fr.)*   An 18th-century name given to light-hearted movements or pieces.

bagatelle *(Fr.)*   A trifle. The name given to little pieces, often for piano, intended to be played for entertainment. However, Beethoven's 27 bagatelles are among the finest works in the piano repertoire.

Balakirev, Mily (1837-1910)   Russian composer, one of the most important 19th-century nationalists. A fine pianist, whose piano works include the brilliant virtuoso 'Oriental fantasy' *Islamey*, together with mazurkas, scherzos, nocturnes and waltzes.

ballade *(Fr.)*   Ballad. A Romantic piece of music, often for piano, in a narrative style, as if telling a story. Chopin and Brahms each wrote four famous ballades.

bar (Amer. **measure**)   A space on the stave divided off by vertical lines, in order to make music easier to read and play.

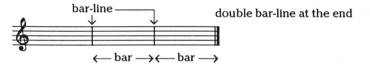

barcarolle   Originally a song sung by Venetian gondoliers, but then adopted as the name for a lilting piano piece in Venetian style. Chopin and Mendelssohn wrote some famous barcarolles for piano.

Barenboim, Daniel (b.1942)   Israeli pianist of Argentinian origin, a pupil of Nadia Boulanger. A child prodigy, Barenboim subsequently enjoyed a brilliant career as a pianist, and later as a conductor. His first wife was the cellist Jacqueline Du Pré.

bar lines   The vertical lines which divide music into regular bars.

Baroque   The name loosely given to the period of musical (and artistic) history between about 1600 and 1750. J.S. Bach and Handel were the most famous composers of the Baroque period; while others included the Italians Alessandro and Domenico Scarlatti, Vivaldi and Corelli; the Frenchmen Lully and Rameau; the Englishman Purcell and the German Schütz.

Bartók, Béla (1881-1945)   Hungarian composer and pianist. He studied in Budapest, and in 1907 became a piano professor at the Academy of Music there. In 1940 he emigrated to the USA. Bartók wrote a great deal of piano music, including 3 important concertos, many transcriptions of Hungarian folksongs, 14 Bagatelles, 3 *Burlesques*, a Sonata and 6 volumes of progressive teaching pieces called *Mikrokosmos*.

bass
(1) The low (bottom) register of music. On the piano, music played with the left hand below middle C.
(2) A male singer with a low voice.
(3) The large string instrument (also known as double bass) with the lowest register.

bass clef   See **clef**.

Béla Bartók

basso continuo *(It.)*   'Continuous bass line'. The name given to the bass part in Baroque music, meant to be played on the harpsichord, supported by a cello, in which only the bass line was written out, with chord progressions indicated by means of figures. The player was then expected to perform a full keyboard part by transforming the figures into appropriate chord sequences. In English, this was known as **figured bass**.

beat   The regular pulse of a piece of music. If there are 4 crotchets in a bar, then there are usually 4 beats in a bar. The beat, however, depends on the speed of the music: if a piece is in 9/8 time, it would have 9 beats in the bar only if played extremely slowly. Such a piece at moderate or fast speed would be more likely to have 3 beats or pulses to a bar, each subdivided into 3 quavers.

Bechstein, Friedrich Wilhelm Carl (1826-1900)   German piano manufacturer, who founded his own firm in Berlin in 1856. Bechstein pianos are rated among the finest concert instruments.

Beethoven, Ludwig van (1770-1827)   German composer, one of the most important in the history of music. Beethoven worked in Vienna, where he made a living as a concert pianist and composer. His piano works, which should form part of every concert pianist's repertoire, include 5 concertos (no.5 is the *Emperor*); 32 sonatas, including the *Pathétique* in C minor, 1799; the *Moonlight* in C sharp minor (1800-1); the *Waldstein* in C major (1804); the *Appassionata* in F minor (1804), *Les Adieux* or the *Lebewohl* in E flat (1809-10) and the *Hammerklavier* in B flat

Beethoven as a young man

(1817-18); 3 sets of bagatelles, and 5 sets of variations, including the *Eroica Variations* (1802) and the massive *Diabelli Variations* (1819-23).

ben, bene *(It.)*   Well; **ben marcato**, well marked.

berceuse *(Fr.)*   Lullaby. Chopin's *Berceuse* in D flat major (1843-4) is one of the best-known examples.

bergamasque *(Fr.)*   A peasant dance from Bergamo in Italy. Debussy used the title in his *Suite bergamasque* for piano (1890-1905).

Bernstein, Leonard (1918-1990)   American composer, conductor, and pianist. Best-known for his stage works, especially the musicals *On the Town*, *West Side Story* and *Candide*, and for his flamboyant career as a conductor. A brilliant pianist, Bernstein specialized in directing

The 1817 Broadwood grand piano owned by Beethoven

concertos from the keyboard. His Second Symphony (*The Age of Anxiety*) contains a long and difficult piano solo in jazz idiom.

bestimmt *(Ger.)*   Decisively.

bewegt *(Ger.)*   Fast-moving.

binary   Term used to describe a piece of music divided into two halves, sometimes contrasting (AB).

Bizet, Georges (1838-1875)   French composer, famous for his opera Carmen and for the incidental music to *L'Arlésienne*. He was also a brilliant pianist, and wrote several piano pieces, including the popular *Jeux d'enfants* (Children's games, 1871) for piano duet (later orchestrated).

'Black-Key' Study   The nickname given to Chopin's *Etude* Op.10 no.5 (published 1833), which uses mainly black notes.

blues   A slow jazz number, originally a song lamenting an unhappy love affair, which characteristically flattens the 3rd and 7th notes of the scale (known as the **blues notes**).

Blüthner   German firm of piano manufacturers, founded in Leipzig in 1853.

B moll *(Ger.)*   B minor.

bolero   A Spanish dance in triple time. Ravel's *Boléro* for orchestra achieved widespread popularity when the ice-skaters Torvill and Dean used it as the basis for one of their routines.

Bolet, Jorge (1914-1990)   American pianist of Cuban origin. Studied at the Curtis Institute, making his début with the Philadelphia Orchestra. One of the finest Liszt interpreters.

boogie-woogie   A jazz style of piano playing, popular in the 1930s, in which the repeated bass line is in split octaves.

Bösendorfer   Viennese firm of piano manufacturers, founded in 1828.

Boulanger, Nadia (1887-1979)   French teacher, conductor and pianist. After an early career as a concert pianist, she devoted her life to teaching, becoming one of the most influential figures in 20th-century music. Pupils included Copland, Lennox Berkeley and Jean Françaix.

Boulez, Pierre (b.1925)   French composer, one of the most important composers, conductors and teachers of his time. A pupil of Messaien, he founded the contemporary music group Domaine musical, and since 1976 has been director of IRCAM (the French government-funded research institute for contemporary music) in Paris. Piano works include 3 important sonatas.

bourrée *(Fr.)*   An old French dance-form, originally a folk-dance from the central and southern regions, which was taken up in the mid-17th century by the French court as a quick dance in duple metre. In the Baroque period, the bourrée became one of the standard dances of the keyboard suite, usually coming after the slow sarabande. It was lively in character, and usually began with a crotchet upbeat. Purcell, Bach and Domenico Scarlatti, among other German, French and Italian composers, wrote keyboard bourrées. Some later composers, including Chabrier and Roussel, wrote bourrées for piano.

brace   The bracket which connects the 2 staves of keyboard music.

Brahms, Johannes (1833-1897)   German composer, one of the most important of the later 'Romantic' period. Worked as concert pianist, and later as conductor in Vienna, where he became director of the famous Gesellschaft der Musikfreunde. In later life he made many international tours as a conductor. His piano works include 2 concertos (in D minor and B flat major); 3 sonatas; 3 sets of variations on themes by Handel (1861), Paganini (1862-3) and Haydn (for 2 pianos, 1873); the *Liebeslieder* Waltzes for piano duet; rhapsodies, studies, scherzos, ballades, capriccios and intermezzos for solo piano; 3 piano quartets; 1 piano quintet and 3 piano trios.

The autograph of Brahms' Intermezzo for piano, Op.118 No.1

branle, bransle *(Fr.)*, **brawl** (Eng.)   A lively peasant round-dance in duple time, taken up by the courts of France and England. The best-known example, from a 16th-century dance treatise, was transcribed by Peter Warlock in his *Capriol Suite*.

bravura *(It.)*   Courage, skill. A bravura passage requires a virtuoso display of brilliant technique.

breit *(Ger.)*   Broadly.

Brendel, Alfred (b.1931)   Austrian pianist, resident in London. One of the most sensitive and thoughtful pianists of his generation, Brendel is renowned for his interpretations of music from the 1st and 2nd Viennese Schools – especially Mozart, Schubert, Beethoven and Schoenberg. He recorded the 1st complete collection of Beethoven's piano works.

breve   The longest value in musical notation, now virtually obsolete. It lasts twice as long as a semibreve, i.e. 8 crotchets.

bridge passage   A short transitional section which links together two more important sections of a substantial piece of music.

Alfred Brendel

brillant *(Fr.)*, **brillante** *(It.)*   Brilliant.

brio *(It.)* Spirit, vigour; **con brio**, **brioso**, with spirit, vigorously.

Britten, Benjamin (1913-1976) English composer, particularly important for his operas, and founder of the Aldeburgh Festival. Though a fine pianist, he wrote little for solo piano except a Concerto, Holiday Diary, and the *Notturno* (Night Piece), written specially for the first Leeds International Piano Competition in 1963.

Broadwood London firm of piano makers, originally founded in 1728. The first Broadwood grand piano was built in 1781. Beethoven owned a Broadwood piano.

broken chord The notes of a chord played one after the other.

Bull, John (*c*.1562-1628) English composer and keyboard player. One of the finest virginals players of his time, Bull worked as organist of the Chapel Royal before leaving England to work for the court at Brussels and at Antwerp Cathedral. Many of his fine keyboard pieces are contained in the publication *Parthenia* (1611).

The Broadwood grand piano used by Chopin on his 1848/9 London visit

burla, burlesca *(It.)*, **burlesque** *(Fr.)* In joking style.

Burgmüller, Johann Friedrich (1806-1874) German composer who settled in Paris after 1832. He wrote many studies for young pianists.

Busoni, Ferruccio (1866-1924) Italian composer, conductor and pianist. Worked mainly in Berlin. His piano works include a concerto in five movements with a male-voice chorus in the finale; 7 *Elegies*, 6 sonatinas, many transcriptions of works by other composers, a book of pieces for children, the *Indian Diary*, and the *Fantasia contrappuntistica* based on Bach.

Buxtehude, Dietrich (Diderik) (1637-1707) Danish organist and composer, one of the greatest organists of his time. From 1668 he was organist at St Mary's Church in Lübeck. The young J.S. Bach walked 200 miles from Arnstadt to Lübeck to hear Buxtehude play.

Byrd, William (1543-1623) English composer of sacred and secular vocal music, and also of music for the virginals. Over 120 pieces of keyboard music survive in collections such as *My Ladye Nevell's Book*, and *Parthenia*.

Ferruccio Busoni

C

C (1) Note name. Middle C, the C nearest the centre of the piano keyboard,

is written  or

(2) **C major, C minor**. The name given to the major or minor scale starting on the note C, and also to the keys based on those scales.

(3) **C clef**. Two different clefs, used for viola or cello music, which fix the position of Middle C. See **clef**.

(4) The sign **𝄴** is a time signature, indicating 4 crotchets to a bar (same as 4/4). Often called 'common time'.

cadence (close) A melodic or harmonic progression which ends a phrase, a section, or an entire piece of music. The most common are the **perfect cadence** (chord V leading to chord I); the **plagal cadence** (chord IV leading to chord I); the **interrupted cadence** (chord V leading to chord VI); and the **imperfect cadence** (chord I or other chord leading to chord V).

cadences in the key of C major

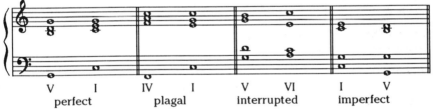

V	I	IV	I	V	VI	I	V
perfect		plagal		interrupted		imperfect	

cadenza *(It.)* A passage, usually of a virtuoso nature, inserted into the closing stages of a piece of music, such as the first movement of a concerto. Originally, the performer was expected to improvise such passages (see **improvisation**), which could last as long as he or she liked. Mozart and Beethoven wrote some, but not all, of their own cadenzas: from Schumann onwards, composers almost always wrote their own.

Cage, John (1912-1992) American composer and pianist, a pupil of Schoenberg. In 1938 he invented the prepared piano, in which various objects were put between the strings to obtain different sound effects. His music makes much use of 'chance' (aleatoric) elements, in which events are left entirely up to the performer. Piano music includes *Music of Changes* (1951), *Music for*

Piano (1952-6), *Cheap Imitation* (1969), *Etude Australis* (32 studies, 1974-5), and pieces for prepared piano such as *Sonatas and Interludes* and *Music for Marcel Duchamp*.

cakewalk   An American ragtime style. Debussy's *Golliwogg's Cakewalk* from his suite *Children's Corner* is one of the best-known examples in piano music.

calando *(It.)*   Dying away.

calmato *(It.)*   Calmed down.

calore *(It.)*   Heat, passion.

canarie *(Fr.)*, **canary** *(Eng.)*   An old dance-form from the Canary Islands, rather like a gigue.

canon   A strict form of counterpoint in which all the parts must follow the melodic and rhythmic pattern laid down by the first part, joining in at regular intervals.

cantabile *(It.)*   In a singing style.

cantilena *(It.)*
    (1) Cradle song.
    (2) A short song.
    (3) Playing in a smoothly flowing, songlike style.

canzona *(It.)*   An instrumental form of the 16th and 17th centuries, in several contrasting sections, which later developed into the sonata. J.S. Bach was one of the last composers to write *canzone*.

capo   See **da capo**.

capriccio *(It.)*, **caprice** *(Fr., Eng.)*   In instrumental music, a light, generally fast piece in free style, almost in the manner of an improvisation. Brahms wrote 7 capriccios.

capriccioso *(It.)*   In a playful style.

Carnaval (Carnival)   21 piano pieces by Schumann, each with a descriptive title (such as *Papillons*), and subtitled 'Little scenes on 4 notes'. The notes A - S - C - H (A flat - E flat - C - B) were taken out of Schumann's own name, and also represented the name of a town where his current girlfriend lived.

Carnaval des animaux *(Fr.,* Carnival of the animals)   A 'grand zoological fantasy' by Saint-Saëns, scored for 2 pianos and chamber ensemble (1886). The 13th of its 14 movements is the famous *Swan*.

Carreño, Teresa (1853-1917)   Venezuelan pianist, a pupil of Gottschalk and Anton Rubinstein. Known as 'The Valkyrie of the Piano' for her power and

brilliant technique, she was one of the greatest female virtuosi of her time. Beautiful and temperamental, she was married four times, once to the pianist and composer Eugen d'Albert.

Casadesus, Robert (1899-1972)   French pianist, born in Paris. He studied at the Conservatoire, and began a career as a touring pianist. In 1941 he settled in the USA. Particularly noted for his interpretations of Mozart, Chopin, Debussy and Ravel. Wife Gaby and son Jean (1927-1972) were also concert pianists.

Catalogue d'oiseaux (List of birds)   A series of piano pieces (1956-8) by Olivier Messaien, based on the calls of 13 different French birds.

cédez *(Fr.)*   Give way, get slower.

cembalo *(It.)*   See **clavicembalo**.

chaconne *(Fr.)*, **ciacona** *(It.)*   A Baroque dance-form, originally from Spain, in triple time, constructed in several sections over a ground bass.

chamber music   Music for a small number of performers, each playing his or her individual part.

chanson *(Fr.)*   Song.

Cherkassky, Shura (b.1911)   Russian pianist, a pupil of the legendary Josef Hofmann. Combines a superb technique with a highly personal style, in a repertoire ranging from the classics to Gershwin.

Shura Cherkassky

Chopin, Fryderyk (1810-1844)   Polish composer and pianist, he worked mainly in Paris, while supporting the nationalist political struggles of his native country. One of the greatest of all composers for the piano, whose music needs great subtlety and insight on the performer's part. Works include 2 concertos, 3 sonatas, 4 ballades, 4 scherzos, 27 *études*, 19 nocturnes, 25 preludes, 14 waltzes, 10 polonaises, 55 mazurkas, and various other genre pieces.

Fryderyk Chopin

Chopsticks (Fr. *Côtelettes* (cutlets); Ger. *Koteletten Walzer*)　A quick waltz for piano, often played by non-pianists either with 2 fingers, or with the sides of the hands, using a chopping motion.

chorale　A hymn-tune of the German Reformed (Lutheran) church. J.S. Bach reharmonized over 400 chorale melodies, and used them in his church music, especially in his chorale preludes for organ.

chorale prelude　An organ composition, popular in Germany during the Baroque period, in which the melody of a chorale was used as the basis of an extended contrapuntal musical composition, often in variation form. J.S. Bach was the supreme master of this type of piece: 46 of his chorale preludes were grouped together in the *Orgelbüchlein*.

chord　Any combination of 2 or more notes played simultaneously. Chords form the basis of musical harmony.

chromatic notes　Notes which do not belong to the diatonic scale. A **chromatic scale** consists of 12 ascending or descending semitones, written in sharps going up, and flats coming down.

Chromatic scale

classical music

(1) A term widely used for 'serious' music, as opposed to 'pop' or 'folk' music.

(2) Music written during the Classical period, c.1750-1820 by Haydn, Mozart, Beethoven, Schubert and their contemporaries.

clavicembalo (*It.*, sometimes abbbreviated to **cembalo**)　Harpsichord.

clavichord　A small early keyboard instrument, with a very soft tone, in which the strings were struck gently, rather than plucked. It was still in use in Bach's time, especially for private practice.

An unfretted Viennese clavichord, 1794, believed to have been owned by Haydn

clavier, Klavier *(Ger.)*   Keyboard.

Clavierübung   See **Klavierübung**.

clef   The symbol placed at the beginning of every line of music to fix the position of the notes on the stave. The **treble clef**, used for the right hand in piano music, and for high notes generally, fixes the note G above middle C on the second line up; the **bass clef**, used for the left hand in piano music, and for low notes generally, fixes the note F below middle C on the second line down. The C or **alto clef**, used for viola music, fixes middle C on the middle line; and the **tenor clef**, used for high cello and bassoon parts, fixes middle C on the second line down.

clefs, showing the position of Middle C

treble clef   bass clef   alto clef   tenor clef

Clementi, Muzio (1752-1832)   Italian pianist and composer, who worked mainly in London, where he founded a music publishing firm and a piano factory. His collection of 100 studies, *Gradus ad Parnassum*, remains a corner-stone of good piano technique. He also wrote over 100 sonatas and sonatinas.

A square piano by Clementi & Co, London 1824

Muzio Clementi

Cliburn, Van (b.1934)   American pianist. In 1958 he became the first American to win first prize in the renowned Tchaikovsky Competition in Moscow, receiving a hero's welcome on his return. Specialized in Russian music, especially Tchaikovsky and Rakhmaninov, and in 1962, founded the Van Cliburn Piano Competition in Texas.

coda *(It.)*   The concluding section of a piece of music.

codetta   a little coda.

Cohen, Harriet (1895-1967)   British pianist, a pupil of Matthay and Busoni. She made her début in 1920, and became famous as a soloist and chamber-music player, specializing in Bach and in contemporary British music – particularly the works of Arnold Bax. In mid-career she suffered an injury to her right arm.

col, colla *(It.)*   With; **colla parte**, 'with the part' – a direction to an accompanist to follow the soloist carefully during a passage in free time.

come *(It.)*   As, like; **come prima**, as at the opening, **come sopra**, as above.

common chord   A triad which includes a perfect 5th (see **interval**). A major common chord includes a major and a minor 3rd; in a minor common chord the lower 3rd is flattened.

common chords in C

major   minor

common time (also known as **perfect time**)   4 crotchet beats to the bar, indicated by the time signature **C** or 4/4

comodo *(It.)*   Comfortable, leisurely.

compass   The range of a voice or instrument, from the highest to the lowest note obtainable.

composition   A piece of music, or the process of writing music.

compound time   Time-signatures in which the beat consists of a dotted note, e.g. 6/8, 9/8).

con *(It.)*   With; **con anima**, with feeling; **con amore**. lovingly; **con brio**, with vigour; **con dolore**, with grief; **con espressione**, with expression; **con forza**, forcefully; **con fuoco**, with fire; **con grazia**, gracefully; **con moto**, with movement; **con sordini**, 'with the mute' – a term used especially by Beethoven to indicate the release of the damper pedal (see **sordino**)

concertante *(It.)*   A work in concerto style, using solo instruments. In Baroque *concerti grossi*, the *concertante* was the group of solo instruments which was contrasted against the main body of the orchestra (the *ripieno*).

concertino *(It.)*
(1) A little concerto.
(2) Same as *concertante*.

concerto   A piece of music for solo instrument, generally accompanied by orchestra.

conjunct motion
The step-by-step progression of a musical line by means of adjacent notes.

consecutive   'Next-door neighbour' (used of notes, or movement by step).

consonance   2 or more notes which, when played together, make a harmonious sound.

continuo   See **basso continuo**.

A piano concerto performance in the late 19th century, conducted by Hans von Bülow

contrapuntal   Relating to counterpoint.

contrary motion   Musical parts which move in opposite directions at the same time.

contredanse   See **country dance**.

Copland, Aaron (1900-1990)   American composer and pianist. Studied in Paris with Nadia Boulanger, later becoming chairman of the Berkshire Music Center. One of the most genuinely 'American' composers. Best-known for his ballets, including *Billy the Kid*, *Rodeo* and *Appalachian Spring*, but piano works include a Concerto (1926), a piano quartet, and a great deal of solo piano music including Variations (1930), a Sonata (1939-41) 4 Piano Blues (1926-47) and a Fantasy (1952-7).

corda *(It.)*   String; **una corda** ('one string'), in piano music, means use the soft pedal, which causes the hammers to strike 1 string instead of the usual 3. Cancelled by the direction **tre corde** ('3 strings').

Cortot, Alfred (1877-1962)   Swiss pianist. Studied at the Paris Conservatoire, where he later taught. He combined the careers of pianist and conductor, and in 1905 founded a famous piano trio with the violinist Jacques Thibaud and the cellist Pablo Casals. As a pianist, Cortot was particularly noted for his Schumann and Chopin, as well as for works by French composers of his own time.

counterpoint   2 or more separate musical lines, played simultaneously, which fit together to form a musical web. The art of combining independent musical lines reached its highest form during the Baroque era, in the works of J.S. Bach and his contemporaries.

countersubject   A device used in fugue, in which another, secondary subject appears, in addition to the main one and its answering phrase.

country dance *(Eng.)*, **contredanse** *(Fr.)*, **contradanza** *(It.)*, **Kontretanz**
(Ger.)   Rustic dances, performed on village greens in Elizabethan times, and then adopted as courtly entertainments. Some, e.g. *Sir Roger de Coverley, The Gay Gordons*, are still performed today in barn dances. Mozart and Beethoven both wrote collections of *Kontretanze*.

Couperin, François (1668-1733)   F r e n c h harpsichordist and composer, who worked at the court of Louis XV. Wrote famous harpsichord method (1716), and published 4 books of harpsichord music containing nearly 230 pieces, often highly ornamented, many with descriptive titles.

François Couperin

couplet
        (1) same as duplet, i.e. 2 notes played in the time of 3.
        (2) The 2-note slur, marked

The second note should be played more lightly and slightly lifted.
        (3) In French 18th-century rondos, the name for an episode.

courante *(Fr.)*, **corrente** *(It.)*   'R u n n i n g'. An old French or Italian dance- form. By the end of the 17th century, there were two distinct types – the lively, flowing Italian *corrente*, in fast triple time (3/4 or 3/8), usually in binary form; and the slower, more stately French *courante*, normally in 3/2 time, and contrapuntal in texture. The courante subsequently formed part of the Baroque suite, often appearing between the allemande and the sarabande. J.S. Bach wrote many examples for keyboard – in all of the English suites, the 1st and 3rd French suites, and the 2nd and 4th keyboard partitas.

Cramer, Johann Baptist (1771-1858) German pianist, composer and teacher, who lived nearly all his life in London. In 1824 he founded a publishing firm, which later began to manufacture pianos. Piano works include 7 concertos, over 100 sonatas, and 84 studies, which are still used for teaching purposes.

crescendo, cresc. *(It.)* Getting   gradually   louder. Also written ⤙

Cristofori, Bartolomeo (1655-1731) I t a l i a n harpsichord-maker working in Florence, where he built the first piano (the forerunner of the modern instrument), in which the strings were struck by hammers, not plucked, and the player could control the dynamic range by means of finger-pressure.

crotchet The quarter-note (♩), i.e. a quarter the length of a semibreve. The crotchet rest is written like this: ⸰

Curzon, Clifford (1907-1982) British pianist, a pupil of Schnabel. He made his début at the Queen's Hall under Sir Henry Wood at 16, and went on to a successful international career. Particularly noted for his interpretations of Beethoven, Mozart and Schubert, but gave some premières of contemporary British works.

Clifford Curzon

Czerny, Carl (1791-1857) Austrian pianist, teacher and composer, pupil of Beethoven and teacher of Liszt. He wrote hundreds of piano works, including sonatas, sonatinas, and many important collections of studies and exercises.

Carl Czerny

D

D (1) Note name.

(2) **D major, D minor**. The name given to the major or minor scales starting on the note D, and also to the keys based on those scales. See also **key** (1).

da capo (*It.*, often abbreviated to **D.C.**)   Repeat from the beginnning; **da capo al fine**, repeat from the beginning as far as the word *fine* (end); **da capo al segno**, repeat from the beginning as far as the sign 𝄋 .

dal segno (*It.*, often abbreviated **D.S.**)   From the sign 𝄋 . **Dal segno al fine**, repeat from 𝄋 as far as the word *fine* (end).

dampers   The felt-tipped levers, part of the action of a piano, which come into contact with the strings after they have been struck, cutting the sound short.

damping pedal   See **piano** (2).

Claude Debussy

Debussy, Claude (1862-1918) French composer. He lived and worked in Paris, but never held any official position, earning a meagre living from his compositions. One of the major composers of piano music, famous for its 'impressionistic' interpretation of sound. Solo piano works include *2 Arabesques* (1888), *Suite bergamasque* (1890-1905), *Pour le piano* (1896-1901), *Estampes* (1903), *L'île joyeuse* (1904), 2 books of *Images* (1905, 1907), 2 books of *Préludes* (1910-13), *Children's Corner* (1906-08), 12 *Etudes* (1915). For piano duet: *Petite suite* (1889); *6 Epigraphes antiques* (1914); for 2 pianos: *En blanc et noir* (1915)

début *(Fr.)*   First public appearance of a soloist.

décidé *(Fr.)*, **deciso** *(It.)*   Decisively.

decrescendo, decresc. *(It.)*   Getting gradually softer.

dehors *(Fr.)*

   (1) Outside; **en dehors**, as if from outside.

   (2) Prominent, e.g. applied to a melody line to be emphasized.

delicato *(It.)*   Delicate; **delicatamente**, delicately.

demisemiquaver   The thirty-second note (♪), half the value of a semiquaver. The demisemiquaver rest is written like this: ♪

descant   A decorative melody played or sung over the top of a main melody, such as a hymn tune.

Deutscher Tanz   See **German dance**.

development   The working-out of the melodic and harmonic material of a previously heard theme, or subject, in order to create new material based on the theme. In sonata form, the development tends to be an extended section lying between the exposition of the principal themes and their recapitulation.

di *(It.)*   Of, from.

Diabelli, Anton (1781-1858)   Austrian composer, and publisher of works by Beethoven, Schubert and Czerny. Wrote piano pieces; responsible for providing the waltz theme on which Beethoven based his 33 *Diabelli Variations*.

diatonic scale   The notes of the scale belonging to a particular major or minor key.

diminished   Reduced. A diminished interval is a perfect or minor interval which is reduced chromatically by one semitone. Usually applied only to 5ths and 7ths. A diminished triad is one where the 5th is reduced by a semitone.

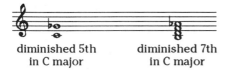

   diminished 5th   diminished 7th
    in C major   in C major

diminuendo, dim. *(It.)*   Gradually getting softer. Also indicated ⟹

diminution   Shortening of the time-values of the notes in a melody or musical line.

di molto *(It.)*   Extremely; **allegro di molto**, extremely fast.

discord, dissonance   A chord which jars the ear, and which needs to be 'resolved' on to one with a more harmonious sound.

disjunct motion   Movement of a musical part by leaps.

dissonance   See **discord**.

divisions   A 17th- and 18th-century form of variation technique, created by decorating the notes of a melody with runs of shorter notes, often improvised.

doch *(Ger.)*   But, yet.

Dohnányi, Ernö (1877-1960)   Hungarian composer and pianist. Piano works include a Concerto; *Variations on a Nursery Song* for piano and orchestra; 4 *Klavierstücke*; 4 Rhapsodies; Variations; Passacaglia.

dolce *(It.)*   Sweet, with a singing tone; **dolcissimo**, very sweet; **dolcemente**, sweetly.

dolente *(It.)*   Sad, sorrowful.

doloroso *(It.)*   Sadly.

dominant   The 5th note of an ascending major or minor scale. A dominant chord is the chord built on this note; a dominant 7th chord is the triad built on the 5th with an extra note – the 7th – added.

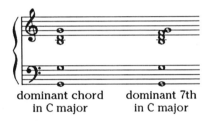

dominant chord   dominant 7th
   in C major   in C major

doppio *(It.)*   Double; **doppio movimento**, twice as fast.

dot

(1) A dot after a note increases its length by half as much again. A second dot after a note (double dot) increases the note by three-quarters of its original value.

(2) A dot over a note indicates that it should be played staccato, i.e. clipped off short.

double *(Fr.)*   A variation.

double bar   The double vertical line which marks off the end of a section of music, or of a whole piece. At the very end, the second line is reinforced.

double-flat   The sign ♭♭ which indicates that the following note should be lowered by a whole tone.

double-sharp   The sign ✗ which indicates that the following note should be raised by a whole tone.

douce, doucement *(Fr.)*   Soft, sweet; softly, sweetly.

duet   Piece for 2 performers. A piano duet is normally a piece for 2 performers on one keyboard (4 hands), but the term can also be applied to music played by 2 performers on separate instruments.

duo *(It.)*   Two. 2 performers, or a piece written for them.

duple time   2 beats in a bar.

duplet   2 notes played in the time of 3. Indicated

Dur *(Ger.)*   Major.

durchkomponiert *(Ger.)*
See **through-composed**.

Dušek (Dussek), Jan Ladislav (1760-1812)
Bohemian pianist and composer who settled in London. Works include 15 piano concertos, 28 piano sonatas.

Dvořák, Antonin (1841-1904)   Bohemian composer, one of the great 19th-century nationalists. After his compositions became internationally renowned, he visited England 9 times and then spent 3 years in the USA as director of the National Conservatory in New York. In 1901 he became director of the Prague Conservatory. Particularly famous for his 9 symphonies. Piano works include a Concerto; 8 Waltzes; 6 Mazurkas; *8 Humoresques*; *Album Leaves*; *Silhouettes*; *Slavonic Dances* for piano duet.

dynamic marks   The signs in music which indicate degrees of loudness or softness. E.g. *ff* or *pp*

Antonín Dvořák

E

E (1) Note name.

(2) **E major, E minor**. The name given to the major and minor scales starting on the note E, and also to the keys based on those scales.

e, ed *(It.)* And.

écossaise *(Fr.)* 'Scottish'. A type of country dance in duple time; the connection with Scotland is unclear. Beethoven and Chopin each wrote several examples.

eighth note *(Amer.)* The quaver.

einfach *(Ger.)* Simply.

élégie *(Fr.)* Elegy: a piece in elegiac mood. Fauré's *Elégie* is one of the most famous examples.

Elgar, (Sir) **Edward** (1857-1934) English composer, one of the major composers of the Edwardian era. Wrote several piano works, including *Concert Allegro*, *Dream Children*, *Skizze*, Sonatina, *Adieu* and Serenade.

embellishment Another name for ornament.

Emperor Concerto The name by which Beethoven's 5th Piano Concerto (1809) is popularly known.

encore *(Fr.)* Again. An extra piece played – at the demand of the audience – at the end of a successful concert.

energico *(It.)* Energetically.

English Suites A set of 6 keyboard suites by J.S. Bach, published after his death.

enharmonic intervals Intervals which change their name, but not their sound, according to how they are written. So C to F sharp would be an augmented 4th, but C to G flat, a diminished 5th.

ensemble *(Fr.)* Together. Any combination of performers. Also used to describe the kind of sound such a group makes.

entrée *(Fr.)* Entrance. An old term for an instrumental piece which introduced an act of a ballet or other stage entertainment. Also used to describe the opening movement of a piece.

episode A section in a piece of music which explores secondary thematic material. It can be used to link larger sections together. In rondo form, the contrasting sections between the returns of the main theme are called episodes.

equal temperament See **temperament**.

Eroica Variations The title given to Beethoven's Piano Variations in E flat major, Op.35 (1802), based on a theme from his ballet *Prometheus* which was also used in the *Eroica* Symphony.

escapement See **piano** (2).

espressione *(It.)* Expression. **Con espressione**, with expression.

espressivo, espress. *(It.)* Expressively.

Estampes (Engravings) 3 piano pieces by Debussy (1903). The individual movements are: *Pagodes* (Pagodas), *Soirée dans Grenade* (Evening in Granada) and *Jardins sous la pluie* (Gardens in the rain).

étude *(Fr.)* Study. Some of the greatest *études* (e.g. by Chopin and Debussy), are really concert pieces.

Études symphoniques (Symphonic studies) A set of 12 variations for piano by Schumann, published in 1837 as his Op.13.

exposition In sonata form, the opening section, in which the principal themes are presented. In fugue, the first statement of the subject by all voices in turn.

expression marks The indications of mood, tempo and dynamics which a composer can put down on paper to help the performer interpret his wishes. Some of the 'expression' is inevitably left up to the individual performer.

extemporization See **improvisation**.

F

F (1) Note name.

(2) **F major, F minor.** The name given to the major and minor scales starting on the note F, and also to the keys based on those scales.

(3) **F clef.** Another name for the bass clef.

f Loud. Abbreviation of **forte**.

ff Very loud. Abbreviation of **fortissimo**.

fff As loud as possible.

fp Loud, then immediately soft. Also an abbreviation of **fortepiano**.

fffp Very loud indeed, followed by an immediate *piano*.

Falla, Manuel de (1876-1946) Spanish composer and pianist, one of the most famous Spanish composers of the 20th century. Piano works include *Nights in the Gardens of Spain* for piano and orchestra (1909-16); *Cuatro Piezas Españolas* (4 Spanish pieces, 1907-8); *Fantasia bética* (1919); Concerto for harpsichord or piano with chamber ensemble (1923-6).

false relation The simultaneous appearance in a chord or in 2 melodic lines of the same note, but in one case sharpened or flattened, and in the other, in its natural state This produces a semitone clash – for instance, between C and C sharp.

fandango *(Sp.)* A lively Spanish dance, either in triple or compound duple time, originally accompanied by guitar and castanets.

fanfare A flourish on trumpets or other brass instruments, announcing an important arrival or entrance.

Fantasiestücke *(Ger.)* Fantasy pieces. Also the name of 8 piano pieces, Op.12, by Schumann (1837-8), each with a descriptive title. Three more (untitled) *Fantasiestücke* were published in 1851 as his Op.111.

fantasy *(Eng.)*, **fantaisie** *(Fr.)*, **fantasia** *(It.)*, **Fantasie** *(Ger.)* Originally, in the 16th century, an instrumental form in several sections, based on a single theme (i.e. an early form of variations). Later (e.g. in the works of J.S. Bach), used as the title of works of an improvisatory character. Schumann, Chopin and later composers used the term for short keyboard pieces of a fanciful nature. Liszt and others wrote 'fantasies' on popular operatic tunes.

Farnaby, Giles (*c*.1560-*c*.1640) English composer. Much of his keyboard music for virginals is contained in the famous collection known as the *Fitzwilliam Virginal Book*.

Fauré, Gabriel (1845-1924)   French composer and organist, pupil of Saint-Saëns, teacher of Ravel. Piano works include 6 impromptus, 13 nocturnes; 13 barcarolles; 4 valse-caprices; Mazurka; *Thème et variations*; 8 *Pièces brèves*; 9 *Preludes*; *Dolly Suite* for piano duet.

feminine ending   The close of a piece in which the final chord arrives on a 'weak' beat of the bar, i.e. not the first.

fermata *(It.)*   Pause, indicated ⌢.

Field, John (1782-1837)   Irish pianist and composer, pupil of Clementi. Settled in Russia. Invented the nocturne, a genre which was shortly afterwards taken up by Chopin. Piano works include 7 concertos, 4 sonatas, 20 nocturnes.

John Field

fifth   An interval made up of 3 whole tones and one semitone (a perfect 5th). A diminished 5th is one semitone smaller; an augmented 5th has an extra semitone. See **intervals.**

figure   A musical motif, or recognizable pattern of notes.

figured bass   See **basso continuo**.

figuration *(It.* **fioritura)**   In piano music, the use of decorative patterns of notes to accompany or ornament a melody.

fin *(Fr.)*, **fine** *(It.)*   End. The word *fine* sometimes appears in the middle of a piece, with an instruction at the end of the score to repeat an earlier section and end at *fine*, e.g. *da capo al fine* – repeat from the beginning as far as *fine*.

finale *(It.)*   The last movement of a work in several movements, such as a sonata.

fingering   The system of indicating, by means of numbers 1 – 5, which finger should be used to play each note or sequence of notes in a piece of keyboard music. Sometimes the composer or editor will indicate the fingering: many performers, especially more advanced ones, prefer to work out a comfortable fingering for themselves.

fino, fin *(It.)*   'As far as'.

first inversion   See **inversion**.

first (second)-time bar   A form of musical shorthand. Where a piece of music has a repeated section which is indicated by means of repeats, rather than written out twice, the ending is often different. A first-time bar, directs the player to complete that bar and return to the beginning. After playing the section through a second time, he or she misses out the first-time bar and goes on instead to the second-time bar:

which leads on in turn to the next section.

Firkušny, Rudolf (b.1912)   Czech pianist. A pupil of Schnabel, he studied at the Prague Conservatory, making his début in 1920. In 1940 he settled in the USA. A champion of contemporary piano music, he gave many premieres of important works by Martin and others.

Fischer, Annie (b.1914)   Hungarian pianist, a pupil of Dohnányi. She made her début at 8, and in 1933 won the Liszt Prize in Budapest. Widely admired for the power and intellectual command of her playing, she was particularly noted for Mozart, Beethoven and Schubert, although her repertory extended from Bach to Bartók.

Annie Fischer

Fitzwilliam Virginal Book   A collection of 297 pieces of English keyboard music, dating from the early 17th century. The original manuscript is kept in the Fitzwilliam Library in Cambridge.

flat

(1) The sign ♭ which, placed in front of a note, lowers its pitch by a semitone. If the key-signature has one or more flats in it, all the appropriate notes in the scale are affected.

(2) To sing or play flat means that the intonation (tuning) is pitched too low.

Flier, Yakov (1912-1977)   Russian pianist, 1st prizewinner at the 1936 Vienna Competition. One of Russia's most celebrated piano teachers, he was a professor at the Moscow Conservatory from 1937 onwards.

folksong   A national song, passed down the ages through being sung, rather than written

extract from the Fitzwilliam Virginal Book

down. In the 20th century, several composers have recorded and notated the traditional folksongs of their own countries. Bartók used many Hungarian folk-tunes in his own pieces, including the *Mikrokosmos* for piano.

form   The structure of a composition, ranging from simple binary or ternary forms, to more complex designs, such as sonata form, rondo, sonata-rondo, or variation form.

forte *(It.*, abbreviated to f)   Loud.

fortepiano *(It.)*
   (1) Same as piano or pianoforte.
   (2) The early version of the piano, used by composers such as Beethoven, Hummel and Schubert.
   (3) The dynamic mark (abbreviated to fp) which tells the player to reduce the level of sound immediately after a loud note or chord.

fortissimo *(It.*, abbreviated ff or, more extremely, fff)   Very loud.

forza *(It.)*   Force; **con forza**, strongly, forcefully.

forzando, forzato *(It.*, abbreviated fz)
See **sforzando**.

fourth   An interval consisting of 2 tones and a semitone (a perfect 4th). An augmented 4th is larger by an extra semitone. See **intervals.**

A Viennese fortepiano by Jacob Bertsche, 1821

Franck, César (1822-1890)   Belgian composer, pianist and, from 1858, organist of the church of Ste Clothilde in Paris. Organ professor at the Paris Conservatoire from 1872. Works include *Organ Symphony* (1886-8); *Variations symphoniques* for piano and orchestra (1885), and several shorter pieces including the *Prélude, chorale et fugue* (1884) and *Prélude, aria et final* (1886-7) for piano, and the *Pièce héroïque* for organ.

Frankl, Peter (b.1935)   Hungarian pianist. He was a pupil of Marguérite Long in Paris, and won many international prizes including the 1958 Liszt Prize. He settled in London in 1962.

French sixth   See **augmented 6ths**.

Frescobaldi, Girolamo (1583-1643)   Italian composer, organist at St Peter's, Rome. Wrote many toccatas, capriccios, fugues and *ricercari* for keyboard.

Froberger, Johann Jacob (1616-1667) German composer and organist, pupil of Frescobaldi. Wrote many toccatas, *ricercari* and fugues for keyboard.

Peter Frankl

fugue   A type of contrapuntal composition (see **counterpoint**) in which several melodic lines or 'voices' enter succesively, imitating each other by following the same pattern of notes. The short motif on which the composition is based is known as the **subject**. The second 'voice' may enter with the subject a 5th higher or 4th lower than the original, in which case it is known as the **answer**, and this pattern may alternate until all the voices have entered. Once this has happened, the **exposition** ends, and a connecting passage or **episode** may occur. Then the subject reappears, followed by more episodes, and so on until the piece ends, often with a **stretto** passage, in which all the voices enter in quick succession, overlapping with each other. J.S. Bach's 2 books of preludes and fugues known as 'The 48', or *The Well-Tempered Clavier* contain 24 masterly examples of keyboard fugues.

fugato *(It.)*   A short passage in fugal style.

fundamental
    (1) The lowest note, or base, of a chord.
    (2) The lowest note of a harmonic series.

fuoco *(It.)*   Fire; **con fuoco**, with fire.

'Funeral March Sonata'   The nickname given to Chopin's B flat minor Piano Sonata, Op.35, because of the famous funeral march in its third movement.

für *(Ger.)*   For. *Für Elise*, Beethoven's famous piano piece, means 'For Elise'.

furiant   A wild Bohemian dance with many changes of rhythm. Dvořák wrote several examples.

furioso *(It.)*   Furiously.

G

G (1) Note name.

(2) **G major, G minor** The names given to the major and minor scales starting on the note G, and also to the keys based on those scales.

(3) **G clef** Another name for the treble clef.

(4) **G.P.** See **General Pause**.

galant Term used to describe the 'courtly' style (*style galant*) of Mozart and Haydn.

galliard A lively dance of the Renaissance period in triple time, which found its way into the early keyboard suite. It was often coupled with the pavan.

galop A fast dance in duple time, developed in 19th-century ballrooms, which was later taken up by by music-hall artistes. The can-can is a type of galop.

Gaspard de la nuit (Gaspard of the night) Set of 3 virtuoso piano pieces by Maurice Ravel, 1908: *Ondine*, *Le gibet* (The gallows) and *Scarbo*.

gavotte An old French dance, originally danced by Breton peasants, and taken up by the French court. It was dignified in character, but quite fast, and either in duple or quadruple metre. By the time it found its way into the Baroque suite as an optional dance, along with popular dances such as the minuet and bourrée, it had become stylized in form, often beginning on the third beat of the bar, and sometimes followed by a **musette**. Many English, French and German composers – including Blow, Purcell, François Couperin, Handel and Bach – wrote gavottes for keyboard, as did a few later composers (Saint-Saëns' *Gavotte* for piano, Op.23 (1872); Schoenberg's *Suite* for piano, Op.25 (1925)).

Gavrilov, Andrei (b.1956) Russian pianist. He studied at the Moscow Conservatory, and has since enjoyed an international career.

gebunden *(Ger.)* Smoothly connected.

gehalten *(Ger.)* Sustained.

General Pause (G.P.) A rest of one or more bars for all players.

German Dance (Deutscher Tanz) A peasant dance from Germany, Austria and Switzerland. Haydn, Mozart and Beethoven all wrote examples.

German 6th   See **augmented 6ths**.

Gershwin, George (1898 - 1937)   American composer. Apart from the opera *Porgy and Bess* and hundreds of popular songs, his best-known compositions are the jazz-influenced Piano Concerto and *Rhapsody in Blue* for piano and orchestra.

geschwind *(Ger.)*   Quickly.

gestossen *(Ger.)*   Short, detached, staccato.

gewidmet *(Ger.)*   Dedicated (to).

Gibbons, Orlando (1583-1625)   English composer and keyboard player, who worked at the court and as organist to Westminster Abbey. His keyboard works number about 40 pieces, some published in *Parthenia* (1611).

Walter Gieseking

Gieseking, Walter (1895-1956)   German pianist. He studied at the Hanover Conservatory, made his début in 1915, and began touring after the First World War. One of the greatest interpreters of the German classics, especially Beethoven, and a champion of Debussy and Ravel.

gigue *(Fr.)*, **giga** *(It.)*, **jig** *(Eng.)*   A lively peasant dance from the British Isles, usually in compound duple or triple time, and with the characteristic

rhythm ♩. ♪♪ . The Fitzwilliam Virginal Book contains early examples of English jigs for keyboard; but by the late 17th century, two distinct types had emerged: the French *gigue*, of moderate to fast tempo, written in 6/4, 3/8 or 6/8 metre, and imitative in texture; and the faster Italian *giga*, homophonic in texture, and often in 12/8 metre. The gigue became enormously popular during the Baroque era, and soon joined the allemande, courante and sarabande as a standard movement of the Baroque suite, often as a finale. Some French composers – and Germans such as Telemann, Handel and J.S. Bach – adopted the Italian form of the dance.

Gilels, Emil (1916-1985)   Russian pianist, a pupil of Neuhaus. In 1938 he won first prize at the Ysaÿe Competition in Brussels, and from that year he taught at the Moscow Conservatory. During the 1950s he began to appear in the West, making his British and American débuts to great acclaim. His repertory ranged from Bach to Bartók, and he was renowned for his flawless technique.

giocoso *(It.)*   Playful.

giusto *(It.)*   Exact, or reasonable. **Tempo giusto** can mean either 'in strict time' or 'at an appropriate speed'.

Glière, Reinhold (1875-1956)   Russian composer, professor at the Moscow Conservatory and teacher of Prokofiev. Works include 175 piano pieces.

Glinka, Mikhail (1804-1857)   Russian composer, founder of the Russian nationalist school of composition. The son of a landowner, he later worked for the Ministry of Communications as a civil servant. Best known for his operas, he also wrote many piano pieces, including waltzes, mazurkas and character pieces.

glissando, gliss. *(It.)*   Sliding. On a keyboard or harp, a glissando effect is made by drawing one finger rapidly up or down an adjacent series of notes or strings. On a bowed instrument like the violin, the same effect is gained by sliding one finger along a string from one note to another. A trombone can also produce a similar effect.

Godowsky, Leopold (1870-1938)   Lithuanian pianist. A child prodigy, he made his début at 9. In 1884 he visited the USA, becoming an American citizen a few years later. He made a triumphant début in Berlin in 1900, and remained in Europe until 1912. Regarded as one of the finest pianists of his generation, particularly noted for his Chopin interpretations. His 53 *études* are modelled on Chopin's.

Goedicke, Alexander (1877-1957)   Russian pianist and composer, professor at the Moscow Conservatory. Wrote numerous small piano pieces.

Goldberg Variations   A set of 30 variations for harpsichord, composed by J.S. Bach at the request of an aristocrat who needed music to lull him to sleep at night. The aristocrat's private harpsichordist, Johann Goldberg, was a former pupil of Bach.

Golliwogg's Cakewalk   The last number in Debussy's piano suite *Children's Corner* (1906-8), written for his daughter. See **cakewalk**.

gopak (hopak)   A lively Russian dance in duple time.

Gottschalk, Louis Moreau (1829-1969) American pianist and composer. Born in New Orleans, he went to Paris in 1842, making his début 3 years later. Studied composition with Berlioz. An amazing virtuoso, Gottschalk had

Louis Gottschalk, a lithograph from 1853

a colourful career, and spent some time in the West Indies. He died of yellow fever in Rio. Wrote many extremely showy and difficult piano pieces.

Gould, Glenn (1932-1982)   Canadian pianist. He made his début at 14, and his American début in 1955. He also toured Europe and the USSR, but retired from the concert platform at the age of 32 to devote himself to recording and broadcasting. His unique Bach interpretations on disc are particularly notable.

grace note   See **ornament.**

Gradus ad Parnassum (Steps to Parnassus)   A collection of 100 piano studies by Clementi (1817); parodied by Debussy in the first piece of his *Children's Corner*, as *Dr Gradus ad Parnassum.*

Glenn Gould

Grainger, Percy (1882-1961) Australian-born pianist and composer, a pupil of Busoni. Collected English folksongs, such as *Molly on the Shore*, and transcribed them for piano, and also for orchestra. Wrote *Country Gardens.*

Granados, Enrique (1867-1916)   Spanish composer and pianist, composer of numerous piano works including 10 Spanish Dances, *Rapsodia Aragonesa*, *7 Valses poeticos*, *Bocetos*, and *Goyescas.*

grandioso *(It.)*   Grandly, in a stately manner.

grand piano   See **piano**.

Grandes études de Paganini (Liszt)   See **Transcendental Studies**.

grave *(It., Fr.)*   Slow and solemn; slower than *lento*, but faster than *largo.*

grazia *(It.)*   Grace; **con grazia**, gracefully.

Percy Grainger

grazioso *(It.)*   Gracefully.

Grieg, Edvard Hagerup (1843-1907)   Norwegian composer, conductor and pianist, one of the nationalist composers whose music was inspired by the scenery and idioms of his native country. Piano works include the famous Concerto in A minor (1868), *4 Pieces*; *4 Humoresques*; *Sketches of Norwegian Life*; *4 Albumblätter*; *Holberg Suite* (later orchestrated for strings); *19 Norwegian Folk Tunes*; *Norwegian Peasant Dances*; *Moods*; 10 books of *Lyric Pieces* (66 pieces in all: no.6 of Book 8 is the *Wedding Day at Troldhaugen*).

Gretchaninov, Alexander (1864-1956)   Russian composer. He worked as a piano teacher in Moscow and St Petersburg before emigrating after the Revolution, first to Paris and then to the USA. He wrote a great deal of piano music, much of it for children (e.g. *Children's Album*; *Grandfather's Album*).

ground bass *(It.* **basso ostinato)**   A short motif or melodic pattern which is constantly repeated in the bass line of a composition, while the upper parts are varied above it. Purcell's aria *When I am laid in earth* (from *Dido and Aeneas*), is one of the most famous examples.

gruppetto *(It.)*   A musical ornament. See **turn**.

Gymnopédies   3 piano pieces by Erik Satie, written in 1888. The title refers to an ancient Greek festival in honour of the god Apollo.

George Frideric Handel

H

H (1) German note name for B natural.

(2) Abbreviation for hand, e.g. L.H., left hand, R.H., right hand.

habañera *(Sp.)* A dance from Cuba, in duple time and with a characteristic dotted rhythm. The most famous example is sung by the heroine in Act 1 of Bizet's opera *Carmen*.

hairpins A name sometimes given to the signs ⎯⎯◁ and ▷⎯⎯ indicating *crescendo* and *diminuendo*.

half note American term for the minim.

half-step American term for the semitone.

'Hammerklavier' Sonata The nickname for Beethoven's Piano Sonata no.29 in B flat major, Op.106. The German word means 'hammer-keyboard', another name for the piano.

Handel, George Frideric (1685-1759) German composer, who worked first in Italy, and then in London, where he became famous as a composer of operas and oratorios, including *Messiah*. His keyboard works consist of 2 sets of 8 suites, published 1720 and 1733, written for his royal pupils.

harmonic minor scale See **minor scale**.

harmonics The natural intervals set up by vibrations of the air when a note is sounded on any instrument. The original note, or first harmonic, is called the 'fundamental': the second harmonic occurs an octave above it; the third harmonic a perfect 5th above that, and so on, gradually diminishing in distance. On a piano, if a note in the bass register is silently depressed and

Fundamental: 𝄞

held down, and another note in the treble register is struck sharply, you should be able to hear the 'harmonic series' ringing faintly.

'Harmonious Blacksmith' A nickname given to the air and variations in Handel's harpsichord suite in E major (1720).

harmonium A small portable reed organ, invented in the early 19th century, and worked by means of air being pumped through pipes by two foot pedals. It has been used in small country churches where no pipe organ is available, and by composers such as Dvořák in his Bagatelles.

A harmonium

harmony The musical texture produced by several notes sounding and moving together at the same time, as a series of chords. The opposite of harmony is counterpoint, in which 2 or more musical lines pursue their own independent paths.

harpsichord An early keyboard instrument, developed during the 15th century and shaped like a wing. When the player depresses a key, a mechanical device called a 'jack' brings a small leather or quill plectrum into contact with the relevant string. Because the strings are plucked, not hit, the sound is more like a lute or guitar than a piano. Before the piano was invented in the 18th century, the harpsichord was the main keyboard instrument, used by every major composer of the time.

A single-manual Venetian harpsichord of 1531

A double-manual harpsichord by Jacob Kirckman, London 1773

Joseph Haydn

Haskil, Clara (1895-1960)   Romanian pianist. A child prodigy, she made her début in Vienna in 1902, and later studied with Cortot and Busoni. Physically small but amazingly powerful, she was noted for her sensitive playing of Mozart, Beethoven and Schubert.

Haydn, Joseph (1732-1809)   Austrian composer, one of the most celebrated of the 'classical' period. He spent much of his life in the service of the Hungarian Esterházy family. After his release from service, he visited England, where his later symphonies were performed. Haydn's unique style, and his pioneering development of forms such as the classical piano sonata and the string quartet had enormous influence on his younger contemporary Mozart, and he was briefly the teacher of Beethoven. His keyboard works include 2 harpsichord concertos and 52 sonatas.

Heller, Stephen (1813-1888)   Hungarian pianist and composer, who studied in Vienna and settled in Paris. He wrote over 100 short piano pieces.

hemidemisemiquaver   The 64th note, a quarter the length of a semiquaver.

Hess, Myra (1890-1965)   British pianist. A pupil of Matthay, she made her début in 1907, and began a career as a touring virtuoso. During the Blitz she organized lunchtime concerts at the National Gallery in London, for which she received the DBE in 1941. She gave many premières of new works by British composers, such as Bliss, Bridge, Bax and Ferguson.

Myra Hess

Hexameron A *pasticcio* made up of 6 piano variations on a march by Bellini, each variation written by a different 19th-century pianist-composer (Liszt, Thalberg, Pixis, Herz, Czerny and Chopin).

Hiller, Ferdinand (1801-1885) German pianist and composer, a pupil of Hummel, and founder of the Cologne Conservatory. His keyboard works include 3 piano concertos and many smaller pieces.

Hindemith, Paul (1895-1963) German composer and teacher. When his music was banned by the Nazi regime, he emigrated to the USA, but returned to Europe after the war. His keyboard works include 3 sonatas; a duet sonata and one for 2 pianos; *Tanzstücke* (1920); Suite (1922); *Klaviermusik* (1925-6); *Ludus Tonalis* (1942); 3 organ sonatas.

Joseph Hofmann aged 10, at the time of his New York début

Hofmann, Josef (1876-1957) Polish pianist, a pupil of Artur Rubinstein. A child prodigy, he made his adult début in Hamburg in 1894, and immediately established an international reputation as a touring virtuoso. From 1898 he lived in the USA, becoming the first director of the Curtis Institute, and where he enjoyed greater success than in Europe. Rakhmaninov dedicated his 3rd Piano Concerto to Hofmann.

homophony *(Gk.)* 'Same-sounding'. A term describing music which sounds chordal because its various 'strands' move together in the same rhythm. Many hymn-tunes are homophonic. See also **polyphony**.

hopak See **gopak**.

hornpipe A British dance, associated with sailors, usually in duple time. Purcell and Handel wrote hornpipes.

Horowitz, Vladimir (1904-1989) Russian pianist. After early studies he left Russia in 1925, making a sensational début in Hamburg with an unrehearsed performance of the Tchaikovsky First Piano Concerto. He made his US début in 1928, and in the 1930s played in a trio with Nathan Milstein and Gregor Piatigorsky. During the 1940s, illness forced his withdrawal from concert life, but in 1951 he returned to the European concert platform, making rare appearances. At 77 he gave two recitals in the Royal Festival Hall in London, to capacity audiences. He was particularly identified with the music of Tchaikovsky, Rakhmaninov and Prokofiev.

Vladimir Horovitz

Horszowski, Mieczyslaw (1892-1993)   Polish pianist. He toured Europe as a child prodigy, before embarking on a career as a soloist and chamber-music player. In 1940 he settled in the USA. At 91, he emerged from retirement to give recitals at the Aldeburgh Festival.

Hummel, Johann Nepomuk (1778-1837)   Austrian pianist and composer, a pupil of Mozart. Worked at various German courts and as touring concert pianist. Works include eight piano concertos, a great deal of chamber music involving piano, and a huge amount of solo piano music, including many sonatas.

humoresque *(Fr.)*, **Humoreske** *(Ger.)*   An instrumental piece of a lively or fanciful nature. Dvořák's *8 Humoresques* for piano are among the most famous examples, as are Schumann's Op.20.

Hungarian Dances   21 piano duets (based on Hungarian idioms) by Brahms, published between 1852 and 1869.

Hungarian Rhapsodies   19 piano pieces by Liszt, which use Hungarian gypsy idioms and rhythms.

hymn   A religious song of praise.

I

Ibéria   4 volumes of piano pieces (12 in all) written 1906-9 by Albéniz. (Also an orchestral work by Debussy).

idyll   A composition of a peaceful type, often describing a country scene.

Images   2 sets of piano pieces (6 pieces in all) by Debussy, written 1905 and 1907: *Reflets dans l'eau* (Reflections in the water), *Hommage à Rameau*, *Mouvement*; *Cloches à travers les feuilles* (Bells through leaves), *Et la lune descend sur la temple qui fût* (And the moon descends on to the former temple), *Poissons d'or* (Golden fish). (Also a set of 3 orchestral symphonic poems by the same composer, completed 1912.)

imitation   A technical device used in composition, in which one instrumental or vocal line repeats a melodic or rhythmic pattern previously stated by another.

impetuoso *(It.)*   Impetuously.

immer *(Ger.)*   Always.

impressionism   The name given to a musical style similar to the technique used by 'impressionist' painters such as Monet, Manet, Renoir and Degas, whereby an image is suggested by blurred shapes and dashes of colour rather than portrayed in a naturalistic manner with clear outlines. Debussy and Ravel were the major musical 'impressionists'.

The Chinese laquerwork which inspired Debussy's 'Poissons d'or'

impromptu *(Fr.)*   Improvised, on the spur of the moment. Short pieces of music, often for piano. Schubert, Chopin and Schumann all wrote impromptus.

improvisation   The term given to music which is made up on the spur of the moment, and played without being written down. Organists and jazz players have always been particularly good at improvising, and it used to be essential for Baroque and early Classical keyboard players, who had to fill in an improvised part from a **basso continuo**. The cadenzas in 18th- and early 19th-century concertos were usually improvised by the soloist.

incalzando *(It.)*   Increasing in tone and speed.

instrumentation   The writing-down of music in a suitable way for various instruments.

instruments, musical   The objects on which people play music. They can be divided into categories according to how they are made or played: stringed instruments; wind instruments; brass instruments; percussion instruments; electronic instruments. The piano is not easily classified: although it has strings, the sound is produced by hammers which strike the strings, so it is really a percussion instrument.

intermezzo *(It.)*   'In between'.

(1) A short movement between other movements in a larger piece of music. The middle movement of Schumann's piano concerto is called 'Intermezzo'.

(2) A short piano piece. Brahms, Schumann and others wrote intermezzos.

interrupted cadence   See **cadence**.

interpretation   The way a particular performer plays a piece of music. Every performance of the same piece can be different: each player will 'interpret' the composer's directions in his or her own individual way after studying the score intensively.

interval   The distance, or difference in pitch, between any two notes. The intervals of a 4th (2 whole tones and one semitone) and a 5th (3 whole tones and one semitone) are called 'perfect' intervals, while all the other intervals in the ascending major scale, measured from the key note, are called **major intervals**. If any major interval is reduced by one semitone, it becomes a **minor interval**: if a perfect or minor interval is reduced by one semitone it becomes a **diminished interval**. If a perfect or major interval is increased by a semitone, it becomes an **augmented interval**.

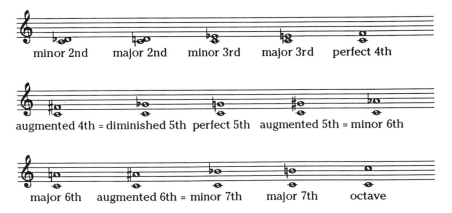

minor 2nd   major 2nd   minor 3rd   major 3rd   perfect 4th

augmented 4th = diminished 5th perfect 5th augmented 5th = minor 6th

major 6th   augmented 6th = minor 7th   major 7th   octave

intonation   Tuning. A performer is said to have 'good intonation' if he or she plays or sings at exactly the right pitch, i.e. 'in tune', and 'bad intonation' ('out of tune') if the pitch is not correct. See also **tuning**.

invention   The name given by J.S. Bach to 15 short keyboard pieces in two parts, which were included in his *Klavierbüchlein* of 1720. Another 15 pieces in 3 parts are known as the 3-part Inventions, although Bach himself called them 'sinfonias'.

inversion   Turning something upside down, e.g. a chord, interval, theme or melody.

Ireland, John (1876-1962)   English composer and pianist. Piano works include a Concerto (1930); *Legend*, for piano and orchestra (1933); Sonata in E minor (1918-20); Sonatina (1926-7); *Decorations* (3 pieces including *The Island Spell*), 1921; 4 Preludes; *Rhapsody*; *3 London Pieces*; *2 Pieces* (*For Remembrance*; *Amberley Wild Brooks*); *Sarnia: An Island Sequence* (1940-41); *3 Pastels* (1941).

Islamey   An 'Oriental fantasy' for piano by the Russian composer Balakirev.

istesso *(It.)*   Same; **l'istesso tempo**, 'the same speed' (even though the value of the beat may have changed, its duration should remain the same).

Italian Concerto   A keyboard composition for two-manual harpsichord by J.S. Bach, published in his *Klavierübung* of 1735.

Italian sixth   See **augmented 6ths**.

Ives, Charles (1874-1954)   American composer and businessman, noted for his highly original and adventurous approach to compositional techniques, which make him one of the first 'avant-garde' composers of the 20th century. Piano works include 3 sonatas (no.2 is the massive and incredibly difficult *Concord* Sonata, which includes solos for flute and viola); over 20 studies; *6 Protests*; *3 Quarter-tone Pieces*.

J

Janáček, Leos (1854-1928)   Czech composer, famous for his operas and for his contribution to the nationalist movement. Piano works include *Vallachian Dances*; *National Dances of Moravia*, for piano duet; *Along an Overgrown Path*, *Sonata 1.x.1905*; *Moravian Dances* (2 books).

jam sessions   The name given to informal sessions during which a group of jazz musicians get together and improvise.

jazz   Name given to a style of black American music, developed in the southern states in the early part of the 20th century, from ragtime (a largely instrumental form), and blues (usually sung). From around 1912 jazz bands became popular, both as smaller ensembles led by a trumpeter such as King Oliver or Louis Armstrong; and later as 'big bands', such as Paul Whiteman's. Duke Ellington was the first great jazz composer. Later forms include 'swing' (1930s), 'be-bop' (1940s), 'cool' jazz and 'free jazz' (1950s and 60s). Many 'serious' composers have used the syncopated rhythms and melodic formulae of jazz, including Debussy, Ravel, Stravinsky, Hindemith, Poulenc, Weill, Berg and Copland.

jig   See **gigue**.

Joplin, Scott (1868-1917) Black American composer and ragtime pianist. His famous piano rags include *The Entertainer*, *Maple Leaf Rag* and *Pineapple Rag*.

jota *(Sp.)*   A lively Spanish dance in triple time, originally accompanied by guitar and castanets.

Joyce, Eileen (1912-1991) Australian pianist. She studied with Matthay and Schnabel, and made her début at the Proms before embarking on a solo career. A popular and glamorous artist, she gave many concerts for British troops during World War II, and later gave the British premières of both Shostakovich concertos.

Eileen Joyce

K

Kabalevsky, Dmitri (1904-1987) Russian composer and pianist. Piano works include 3 concertos, 3 sonatas, 4 Preludes (1927-8); 24 Preludes (1943-4); *4 Little Pieces*; *15 Children's Pieces*; *24 Little Pieces*; *5 Easy Variations*; 4 Rondos.

Kalkbrenner, Friedrich (1785-1849) German pianist and composer. He studied at the Paris Conservatory, and then toured Europe before settling in Paris as a teacher and virtuoso. Chopin dedicated his First Concerto to Kalkbrenner. Piano works include 4 concertos, 15 sonatas and a great deal of chamber and solo keyboard music.

Kawai A Japanese firm making grand and upright pianos.

Kempff, Wilhelm (1895-1991) German pianist. Studied in Berlin, and became particularly noted for his poetic Beethoven and Schumann interpretations.

Kentner, Louis (1905-1987) Hungarian pianist, who settled in Britain in the 1930s. A noted champion of contemporary music, including works by Bartók, Bliss, Rawsthorne and Tippett.

key
  (1) A piece is said to be in a particular 'key' if its musical material predominantly uses the notes of the same scale, either major or minor. So the first prelude and fugue in Bach's keyboard collection known as 'The 48', is 'in C major'.
  (2) The lever on a musical instrument, such as a key on a piano, which, when pushed by a finger or a foot, helps to produce a note on that instrument.

keyboard
  (1) The set of keys on a particular instrument.
  (2) A general term given to works which may be played on certain keyboard instruments, such as piano, organ or harpsichord.

key-note The tonic note of a particular scale.

key-signature The symbol, expressed either in sharps (♯) or flats (♭) which is placed at the head of every stave of music, after the clef, to tell the player which key he or she is playing in. The order of the sharps in key-signatures is by rising 5ths, and of flats by falling 5ths.

Khachaturian, Aram (1903-1978) Armenian composer, famous for the ballet *Spartacus*, a movement from which was used as the theme tune to the TV series *The Onedin Line*. Piano music includes a Concerto, a Sonata, a Sonatina, *7 Recitatives and Fugues*, Suite, and 3 Marches.

Kinderszenen (Scenes from Childhood)   A set of 13 pieces by Schumann, Op.15 (1838), of which no.7 is the famous *Träumerei*.

Klavier *(Ger.)*   Keyboard.

Klavierbüchlein (Little keyboard book)   The title given by J.S. Bach to 3 collections of his keyboard music, including one set of pieces for his eldest son, Wilhelm Friedemann and two for his second wife, Anna Magdalena.

Klavierstück *(Ger.*, pl. **Klavierstücke**)   Piano piece(s).

Klavierübung (Keyboard exercise)   The title given by J.S. Bach to a 4-part collection of keyboard works, containing 6 partitas or German suites, 1731; the *Italian Concerto* and Partita in B minor; organ works including the *St Anne* Fugue, and the *Goldberg Variations*. The title *Klavierübung* was first used by Bach's predecessor at Leipzig, Johann Kuhnau.

Köhler, Christian Louis (1820-1886)   German piano teacher and composer of numerous piano studies.

Konzertstück *(Ger.*, pl. **Konzertstücke**)   Concert piece. A title often applied to short concerto-like pieces for solo instrument and orchestra, such as Weber's *Konzertstück* for piano and orchestra.

Kovacevich, Stephen (formerly Stephen Bishop) (b.1940) American pianist, who settled in Britain and studied with Myra Hess. Now a world-famous touring concert pianist. Richard Rodney Bennett's Piano Concerto is dedicated to him.

kräftig *(Ger.)*   Energetically.

Kreisleriana   Set of 8 fantasy pieces by Schumann (1838), based on a character in the fantastical stories of E.T.A. Hoffmann, and dedicated to Chopin.

Kuhlau, Friedrich (1786-1832) German-born composer and pianist, a friend of Beethoven, who worked as a concert pianist and as composer to the Danish court. He is best known for his piano music, which

Stephen Kovacevich

includes a Concerto (1810) and many teaching pieces, including some well-known sonatinas.

Kuhnau, Johann (1660-1722)   Bohemian composer, cantor at the church of St Thomas, Leipzig, immediately before J.S. Bach. Published 4 sets of keyboard music – 2 sets each of 7 suites entitled *Klavierübung*, and two sets of sonatas – he was one of the earliest composers to write keyboard sonatas. The last set, *Biblischer Historien*, is a set of programme sonatas illustrating biblical stories.

kurz *(Ger.)*   Short.

L

Katia and Marielle Labèque

L Abbreviation for left, as in L.H., left hand.

Labèque, Katia (b. 1953) and **Marielle** (b.1956) French pianists. Studied at the Paris Conservatoire, each graduating with a 1st prize the same year. Since 1961 they have pursued a highly successful international career as a piano duo, with a wide-ranging repertoire including jazz.

lacrimoso, lagrimoso *(It.)*   Sad, tearful.

laisser vibrer *(Fr.)*   'Let it vibrate', i.e. allow the sound to ring on and die away gradually, not lifting the piano key or raising the sustaining pedal.

lament *(It.* **lamento**)   A piece of sorrowful music expressing grief.

Ländler *(Ger.)*   A rustic slow waltz from Austria. Beethoven and Schubert both wrote *Ländler*.

Landowska, Wanda (1877-1959) Polish pianist and harpsichordist. Taught in Berlin and Paris before settling in the USA. One of the great pioneers of the harpsichord revival, noted for her Bach interpretations. Manuel de Falla and Francis Poulenc both wrote harpsichord concertos for her.

Wanda Landowska

langsam *(Ger.)*   Slow.

largamente *(It.)*   Broadly, in a dignified manner.

larghetto *(It.)*   Slow and dignified, but faster than *largo*.

largo *(It.)*   Broad, slow and stately.

Larrocha, Alicia de (b.1923)   Spanish pianist. She made her début at 5, and her adult début in 1940. Since 1947 she has toured the world as a concert pianist.

leading-note   The seventh note of an ascending major scale, which 'leads' upwards to the tonic.

'Lebewohl, Das' *(Ger.)*, **'Les Adieux'** *(Fr.)*   'The Farewell'. Beethoven's own name for his Piano Sonata No.26 in E flat major, Op.81a, written to commemorate the exile from Vienna of his patron, the Archduke Rudolf, during the Napoleonic invasion.

lebhaft *(Ger.)*   Lively.

ledger (or **leger**) **lines**   Short lines written above or below the stave to accommodate notes which are too high or low to fit on the stave itself.

legato *(It.)*   Smooth, seamless performance with no gaps between consecutive notes, indicated by a slur or a curved phrase mark over the passage concerned. The opposite of staccato.

léger *(Fr.)*   Light.

leggero, leggere *(It.)*   Light; **leggeramente**, lightly; **leggerissimo**, as light as possible.

legglero *(It.)*   Light; **leggieramente**, lightly.

leicht *(Ger.)*   Light.

leise *(Ger.)*   Lightly, softly.

lent *(Fr.)*, **lento** *(It.)*   Very slow; **lentement** *(Fr.)*, **lentamente** *(It.)*, very slowly.

Leschetitzky, Theodor (1830-1915)   Polish pianist. A pupil of Czerny, he worked in Russia, where he taught at the St Petersburg Conservatory. In the 1880s he settled in Vienna. One of the greatest piano teachers of all time, his pupils included Horszowski, Moisiewitsch, Paderewski, Schnabel and Wittgenstein.

Lhevinne, Josef (1874-1944)   Russian pianist. He was a fellow-pupil of Rakhmaninov at the Moscow Conservatory, and made his début in 1899 under Artur Rubinstein, and his US début in 1906. In 1919 he and his wife Rosina emigrated to the USA, where they toured and taught at the Juilliard School. Regarded as one of the great virtuosi.

Lhevinne, Rosina (1880-1976)   Russian pianist, wife of Josef Lhevinne. Made her Moscow début in 1895 and her US début in 1923. Like her husband, a celebrated pianist and teacher.

lied *(Ger.)*   Song.

Lied(er) ohne Worte *(Ger.)*   Song(s) without words. Title given by Mendelssohn to 48 short piano pieces contained in 8 published volumes, 1832 - 45. All have a songlike melody against a flowing accompaniment.

Lill, John (b.1944)   British pianist. Studied at the Royal College of Music. making his London début in 1963. In 1970 he won joint 1st prize at the Tchaikovsky Competition. Particularly noted as a fine Beethoven interpreter.

Lipatti, Dinu (1917-1950)   Romanian pianist, a pupil of Cortot. Began his concert career in 1939, settled in Switzerland 1943. Died of leukaemia. Noted for his performances and recordings of the romantic repertoire, especially Schumann and Chopin.

l'istesso tempo *(It.)*   See **istesso**.

Liszt, Franz (or **Ferencz**) (1811-1886)   Hungarian composer and pianist, one of the greatest virtuoso pianists of all time. A pupil of Czerny, he was Kapellmeister at the Weimar court 1848-59, before moving to Rome, where he took holy orders in 1865. His later years were spent touring and teaching. Piano works include 2 Concertos; *Hungarian Fantasia, Todtentanz,* Fantasia on themes from Beethoven's *Ruins of Athens* and *Rapsodie espagnole* for piano and orchestra; *Album d'un voyageur* (9 pieces, 1852); 3 books of *Années de pèlerinage* (Pilgrimage years), containing 26 pieces (no.6 of Book 1 is *La vallée d'Obermann*, no.7 of Book 2 is the *Dante* Sonata, no.4 of Book 3 is *Les jeux d'eau à la Villa d'Este*); *Consolations* (1850); 2 Concert Studies; *Funérailles* (1850); *Etudes d'exécution transcendante* (Transcendental Studies); 2 *Légendes*; 3 *Liebesträume*; 3 *Mephisto Waltzes*; 4 *Valses oubliées*; 19 *Hungarian Rhapsodies*; Sonata in B minor (1854).

Liszt playing to friends (Berlioz and Czerny standing)

Litolff, Henry (1818-1891)   British pianist and composer, a pupil of Moscheles. Made his début at 12. Toured Europe before settling in Brunswick, where he ran a music publishing business. The Scherzo of his 4th Piano Concerto is still often played.

loco *(It.)*   Place. A term used after a performer has been directed to play an octave higher or lower than written, to remind him or her to play once more at the written pitch.

Long, Marguérite (1874-1966)   French pianist. A pupil of Marmontel at the Paris Conservatoire, she became a noted exponent of French music, especially Fauré, Debussy and Ravel. Ravel dedicated his G major Concerto to her.

lontano *(It.)*   Distant; **a lontano**, in the distance; **come da lontano**, as if from a distance.

Loriod, Yvonne (b.1924)   French pianist, 2nd wife of Olivier Messaien. A noted exponent of contemporary music, she has given premières of many works by Bartók, Messaien and others. The piano part of the *Turangalîla Symphony* was written for her.

loud pedal   Another name for the sustaining pedal.

louré *(Fr.)*   An old French dance, like a slow jig.

Ludus tonalis (Note-play)   Studies in counterpoint and piano playing by Hindemith (1942), consisting of a prelude, 12 fugues with interludes, and a postlude.

lunga pausa *(It.)*   A long rest.

Lupu, Radu (b.1945)   Romanian pianist. He made his début at 12 and studied at the Moscow Conservatory. In 1966 he won 1st prize in the Van Cliburn Competition and, in 1969, 1st prize at Leeds, which launched an international career. Now lives in Britain, making rare public appearances. Noted for his interpretations of the Classical and Romantic repertory.

lusingando *(It.)*   Flattering, wheedling; i.e. play in a coaxing manner.

lustig *(Ger.)*   Cheerful.

lyric   A short poem, or the words of a song. Grieg gave the title *Lyric Pieces* to several of his shorter, songlike compositions.

Radu Lupu

M

ma *(It.)*   But.

MacDowell, Edward (1861-1908)   American composer and pianist. He studied in Germany, and met Liszt. First head of music at Columbia University, New York. Piano works include 2 concertos, 4 sonatas (*Tragica, Eroica, Norse, Keltic*), 12 Virtuoso Studies, 10 *Woodland Sketches* (no.1 is *To a wild rose*), *2 Modern Suites, Forest Idyls, 6 Idyls after Goethe, 8 Sea Pieces, 6 Fireside Tales, 10 New England Idyls.*

maestoso *(It.)*   Majestic, in a dignified manner.

maestro *(It.)*   Master. The title given to famous musicians, especially composers, teachers or conductors. In the USA the title nearly always means a conductor.

main droit *(Fr.)*, **mano destra** *(It.,* abbreviated **M.D.**)   Right hand.

main gauche *(Fr.,* abbreviated **M.G.**)   Left hand.

major chord   A chord which includes a major 3rd (i.e. an interval made up of two whole tones from the tonic note).

major scale   An 8-note scale made up of intervals of a whole tone, except for degrees 3-4 and 7-8, which are semitones.

mancando *(It.)*   Fading away.

mano sinistra *(It.,* abbreviated **M.S.**)   Left hand.

manual   The keyboards (played with the hands) of an organ or harpsichord.

marcato *(It.)*   'Marked'. Each note is given a heavy emphasis.

march *(Fr.* **marche**, *Ger.* **Marsch**, *It.* **marcia**)   The rhythmic sort of music which accompanies a group of people, such as soldiers, marching in step. Schubert's *Marche militaire* for piano duet is a good example. **Tempo di marcia**, in march time.

markiert *(Ger.)*   Marked.

martellato *(It.)*   Hammered, forceful.

Martinů, Bohuslav (1890-1959)   Czech composer and violinist. He studied at the Prague Conservatory, worked in Paris from 1923 to 1941, then left for the USA, finally returning to Europe in 1953. Piano works include 5 concertos, a Concertino and a Double Piano Concerto, and many short piano pieces, including three books entitled *Loutky* (Puppets, 1912-24).

marziale *(It.)*   In martial style.

mässig *(Ger.)*   Moderately. **Mässig bewegt**, moderately fast.

Matthay, Tobias (1858-1945)   English pianist and teacher, professor of piano at the Royal Academy of Music from 1880. Pupils included Myra Hess, Harriet Cohen and Fanny Waterman.

mazurka   A wild and lively Polish country dance in triple time, based on repeating rhythmic patterns, and with characteristic dotted rhythms accentuating the second beat of the bar. It was originally danced by 4, 8 or 12 couples. By the 17th century the mazurka had spread into neighbouring countries, and by the early 19th century it had reached England. Chopin wrote about 50 mazurkas for piano, which are regarded as the highest achievements in the genre. In his hands the mazurka could express extremes of joy or sorrow. His example was followed by the Polish composer Karol Szymanowski, while several notable Russian composers wrote piano mazurkas, including Borodin (*Petite Suite*), Glinka and Tchaikovsky.

M.D.   Abbreviation for **main droit** *(Fr.)*, **mano destra** *(It.)* Right hand.

measure   The American term for bar.

mediant   The 3rd note of the scale.

melodic minor scale   See **minor scale**.

mélodie *(Fr.)*   Song, or lyrical piece in songlike style.

melody   A succession of notes, moving in any direction either by step (conjunct motion) or by leaps (disjunct motion), which makes up a recognizable tune. The title is sometimes given to a short, simple piece, such as Rubinstein's *Melody in F* for piano.

Mendelssohn, Felix (1809-1847)
German composer, pianist, organist and conductor. An extraordinarily gifted child, Mendelssohn began composing at an early age - at 17 he wrote the overture to *A Midsummer Night's Dream*. Became conductor of the Leipzig Gewandhaus orchestra, and then first director of the Leipzig Conservatory. Piano works include 2 concertos (G minor, D minor), *Capriccio brillant* in B minor, *Rondo brillant* in E flat, both for piano and orches-

Felix Mendelssohn

tra; 3 sonatas, *7 Characteristic Pieces*; *Rondo capriccioso*; 8 books of *Songs Without Words*; 3 Capriccios; *Variations sérieuses* in D minor; Variations; 3 Preludes; 3 Studies. Organ works include 6 sonatas; 3 Preludes and Fugues; *Andante and Variations* in D.

meno *(It.)*   Less; **meno mosso**, 'with less movement', i.e. slower; **poco meno mosso**, a little slower; **meno allegro**, less fast.

menuet *(Fr.)*, **Menuett** *(Ger.)*   See **minuet**.

Messaien, Olivier (1908-1992)   French composer, organist and teacher, one of the most influential 20th-century composers. Studied at the Paris Conservatoire, also studied Indian and Greek music. From 1931 he was organist at La Trinité in Paris, and from 1942 he taught at the Paris Conservatoire. Many of his works make use of birdsong imitations (he notated the songs of all French birds), and most were inspired by his deep religious faith. Piano works include *8 Préludes, Fantaisie burlesque*; *Visions de l'Amen*; *Vingt regards sur l'enfant Jésus*; *Quatre études de rhythme, Catalogue d'oiseaux* (Bird catalogue). Organ works include *L'Ascension*; *La Nativité du Seigneur, Les Corps glorieux*; *Messe de la Pentecôte*; *Livre d'orgue*; *Méditations sur le mystère de la Sainte Trinité*.

mesto *(It.)*   Sad.

metre *(Amer.* **meter***)*   The name given to the regular succession of pulses or beats which underlie the rhythms of notes in a bar, e.g. 2/4 or 6/8.

metronome   A mechanical device which sets a regular metrical pulse, either by ticking (the clockwork variety), or by an electronic signal (the digital variety). The device can be set to produce a wide range of beats per minute, and can be used either to establish the pulse according to the composer's instructions, e.g. M.M. ♩ = 60 (60 crotchet beats per minute), or, for learners, to help them keep a particular passage strictly in time. The metronome was patented in the early 19th century by the German inventor Johann Nepomuk Maelzel (a friend of Beethoven), who gave his name to it.

mezzo, mezza *(It.)*   Half; **mezzo-forte**, half-loud; **mezzo-piano**, half-soft.

mf   Abbreviation for **mezzo-forte** *(It.)*, 'half-loud', i.e. moderately loud. Beethoven used this dynamic only twice in his piano sonatas, in the last movement of Op.2 no.2 in A major, and in the first movement of Op.101, also in A major.

M.G.   Abbreviation for **main gauche** *(Fr.)*, left hand.

Michelangeli, Arturo Benedetti (b.1920)   Italian pianist. In 1939 he won 1st prize at the Geneva International Competition. After the Second World War he began touring and recording, establishing a reputation as one of the greatest virtuosi of his time. Particularly associated with the music of Mozart,

Debussy and Ravel.

Middle C   The C nearest the middle of the piano keyboard.

Mikrokosmos   The title given by Bartók to a set of 153 'progressive pieces' for piano, many based on folk-tunes, composed between 1926 and 1939 and published in 6 volumes.

minaccevole *(It.)*   Menacing.

minim *(Amer.* **half-note)**   The note ♩ which lasts 2 crotchet beats, i.e. half a semitone. The minim rest is written like this ▬

minor intervals   See **interval**.

minore *(It.)*, **mineur** *(Fr.)*   Minor.

minor key   A key based on the appropriate minor scale (see next entry).

minor scale   A scale in which the 3rd note is flattened. In the **harmonic minor scale**, the 6th note is also flattened both going up and coming down, producing the interval of an augmented 2nd between the 6th and 7th notes. In the **melodic minor scale**, the 6th remains normal going up, but coming down, both it and the 7th are flattened.

Harmonic minor scale of C

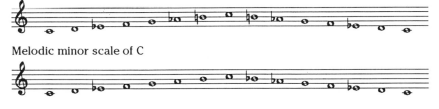

Melodic minor scale of C

minstrel
    (1) A medieval troubadour, or a wandering singer or player.
    (2) A performer who 'blacks-up' (paints his face and hands black) to imitate the look and music of 19th-century American negro musicians. This type of entertainment used to be popular in music-halls, but has fallen out of fashion. Debussy's piano prelude *Minstrels* parodied such entertainers.

minuet *(Eng.)*, **menuet** *(Fr.)*, **Menuett** *(Ger.)*, **minuetto** *(It.)*
A graceful dance in moderate triple time, originally performed by French peasants,but taken up by the court in the 17th century. Composers soon began to write minuets, and the dance became an optional movement in the Baroque suite. In the 18th century it became a standard movement in the symphony, where it was usually the 3rd of 4 movements. The minuet normally has 2 repeated sections of equal length, plus a middle section in contrasting style, called a 'trio' because it is normally in 3-part harmony. Many trios also

have 2 repeated sections, and then the minuet is played again, without repeats, to complete the piece.

'Minute Waltz'   The nickname given to Chopin's Waltz in D flat, Op.64 no.1, which is supposed to be able to be played within one minute – but only if it is played too fast!

Miroirs (Mirrors)   A set of 5 piano pieces by Ravel, composed in 1905. The pieces are: *Noctuelles, Oiseaux tristes, Une barque sur l'océan, Alborado del grazioso, La vallée des cloches.*

mirror canon, mirror fugue   A canon or fugue in which the parts appear at the same time both the right way up and upside down, as if reflected in a mirror.

misterioso *(It.)*   Mysterious.

misura *(It.)*   Measure (of tempo); **senza misura**, in free time (without a beat).

M.M.   Abbreviation for Maelzel's Metronome. See **metronome**.

mit *(Ger.)*   With.

moderato *(It.)*   At a moderate speed.

modes   The 12 scales which were used in European music from about 400-1500 AD. Of these, 4 can be found by playing the 8 white keys of the piano starting on notes D, E, F and G (these were known as the **authentic modes**). 4 more (the **plagal modes**) used the same notes, but started on the dominant (the fifth note) of the authentic modes, i.e. A, B, C and D. A further 4 were then created by adding the authentic modes beginning on A and C, together with their plagal forms, starting on E and G. In 1547 the Swiss monk Henricus Glareanus gave all 12 modes Greek names, as follows:
I **Dorian**; II **Hypodorian**; III **Phrygian**; IV **Hypophrygian**; V **Lydian**; VI **Hypolydian**; VII **Mixolydian**; VIII **Hypomixolydian**; IX **Aeolian**; X **Hypo-aeolian**; XI **Ionian**; XII **Hypoionian**
Eventually the system of modes gave way to the present-day major and minor scales, which are based respectively on the Ionian and Aeolian modes. Some 20th-century composers, such as Debussy, Ravel, Stravinsky, Bartók and Vaughan Williams, have used the old modes to create **modal harmony**, which also survives in folksong.

modulation   Moving from one key to another during the course of a piece. The simplest modulations are to related keys, such as the relative major or minor, the dominant or subdominant.

Moisewitsch, Benno (1890-1963)   Russian pianist, a pupil of Leschetizky. Settled in Britain after his début in 1908, and toured worldwide. During the Second World War, gave many concerts for the *Aid to Russia* Fund.

moll *(Ger.)*   Minor.

molto *(It.)*   Very; **allegro molto**, very fast.

Moment musical *(Fr.)*   'Musical moment'. The title sometimes given to short piano pieces in the 19th century, such as Schubert's 6 **Moments musicaux** (1827).

'Moonlight' Sonata   The nickname of Beethoven's popular Piano Sonata no.14 in C minor, Op.27 no.2 (1800-01). The name became attached because a poetic reviewer wrote that the first movement reminded him of moonlight on Lake Lucerne.

Moore, Gerald (1899- 1987)   British pianist, one of the most distinguished accompanists of his time. Partners included Victoria de los Angeles, Elisabeth Schwarzkopf, Dietrich Fischer-Dieskau.

morceau *(Fr.)*   Piece. Satie's *3 morceaux en forme de poire* (3 pear-shaped pieces) for piano duet, written in 1903, actually consist of 6 pieces.

mordent   An old ornament, like a very short trill, often found in keyboard music. The **upper mordent** (**Pralltriller** in German) is written like this:

 and played like this:

while the **lower mordent** (**Mordent** in German) is written like this:

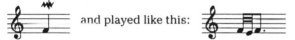 and played like this:

morendo *(It.)*   'Dying away'. Getting softer.

Moscheles, Ignaz (1794-1870)   German/Bohemian pianist and composer. Studied in Vienna and then became touring concert pianist. Settled in London, 1826; professor at Leipzig Conservatory from 1846. Piano works include 8 concertos, 6 sonatas (2 for duet), 24 studies, 50 preludes, *12 Characteristic Studies*, 59 *Daily Studies* for duet.

mosso *(It.)*   'Moved'; **più mosso**, 'more moved', i.e. quicker.

Moszkowski, Moritz (1854-1925)   Polish/German pianist and composer, mainly remembered for his charming *Spanish Dances* for piano duet.

motif *(Fr.)*; **motive** *(Eng.)*; **Motiv** *(Ger.)*   The shortest rhythmic or melodic figure which makes sense by itself, such as the 4 notes which open Beethoven's Fifth Symphony.

motion
    (1) The direction in which a melody progresses. If 2 parts or voices of a contrapuntal composition proceed in the same direction, that is called **similar**

motion, if in opposite directions, that is **contrary motion**. If 2 parts proceed in the same direction, keeping exactly the same distance apart, that is **parallel motion**.

(2) In a single musical line, if one note progresses by step to its next-door neighbour, that is called **conjunct motion**; if it leaps to another note, that is **disjunct motion**.

moto *(It.)*   Motion; **con moto**, with motion, i.e. swiftly flowing; **moto perpetuo** *(It.)*, perpetual motion, i.e. a piece in which the movement is continuous, in rapid notes.

mourant, en mourant *(Fr.)*   Dying.

mouvement *(Fr.)*   Movement.
(1) Motion.
(2) See **movement**.
(3) A term used by some French composers such as Debussy to indicate a return to the original speed after some fluctuation of tempo.

mouvement perpetuel *(Fr.)*, **moto perpetuo** *(It.)*   Perpetual motion. See **moto**.

movement   An independent section of a larger piece, such as a sonata, symphony, suite or concerto. Individual movements are usually contrasting in character, with separate tempo indications. Some large-scale pieces, such as Schubert's *Wanderer Fantasy* for piano, are in one continuous movement, not subdivided.

Mozart, Wolfgang Amadeus (1756-1791)   Austrian composer and pianist, one of the world's greatest composers. Born in Salzburg, he toured Europe as a child with his family (his elder sister was also a fine keyboard player), making 2 trips to Italy where his youthful operas were performed. In 1781 he left the service of the Archbishop of Salzburg to work as a freelance pianist/composer in Vienna. Though successful at first, producing a brilliant series of piano concertos and operas, he never achieved financial security, and died in relative poverty at the early age of 35. Piano works include 29 concertos, 17 sonatas and numerous other shorter works, including 13 sets of variations, the Fantasia in C minor, and the Rondo in A minor.

mp   Abbreviation for **mezzo-piano** *(It.)*, 'half-soft'.

MS   Manuscript; **MSS**, manuscripts.

M.S.   Abbreviation for **mano sinistra** *(It.)*, left hand.

Müller, August Eberhard (1767-1817)   German conductor, pianist and composer. A pupil of J.C.F. Bach, he worked in Berlin, Leipzig and Weimar. His keyboard works include an influential tutor; 2 concertos; 17 sonatas; around 20 caprices; 6 sets of variations.

Mulliner Book   A collection of 131 pieces, mainly for keyboard, made around 1560 by Thomas Mulliner. One of the most important sources of early English keyboard music.

munter *(Ger.)*   Lively.

musette *(Fr.)*
   (1) A 17th-century French bagpipe.
   (2) A dance movement, rather like a gavotte, except that it has a drone bass which imitates the sound of the bagpipe. The musette was often paired with the gavotte as an optional movement of the Baroque suite.

Mussorgsky, Modest (1839-1881)   Russian composer, a pupil of Balakirev, and one of the 'Mighty Handful' of 19th-century nationalist Russian composers. Best-known for his opera *Boris Godunov*. Piano works include *Souvenir d'enfance* (Memory of childhood); *Intermezzo*; *Pictures at an Exhibition* (1874)

mute   A mechanical device used to make the sound of an instrument softer. On the piano, the sound can be muted by using the left (soft) pedal.

The Mozart family in 1780: Wolfgang and his sister Nannerl are at the keyboard

N

Nachtmusik *(Ger.)*　Night music. Music to be played in the evening or at night.

Nachtstück *(Ger.)*　A piece which creates the atmosphere of night. See **nocturne**.

natural
　　(1) A note which is neither raised (sharpened) nor lowered (flattened).
　　(2) The sign (♮) which restores a note to its original pitch, after it has been sharpened or flattened.

naturale *(It.)*　The term which directs performers to return to a natural or normal style of playing, after being instructed to do something unusual.

Neapolitan 6th　A type of chromatic chord, consisting of the first inversion of the major common chord based on the flattened supertonic. In the key of C major, the Neapolitan 6th would look like this:

neo-classical　The term given to some 20th-century music written in imitation of the Classical style, such as Prokofiev's *Classical Symphony*. Some of Stravinsky's music is neo-classical.

nicht *(Ger.)*　Not.

niente *(It.)*　Nothing; **al niente**, dying away to nothing.

Nikolaeva, Tatiana (b.1924) Russian pianist, one of the most distinguished of her generation. Particularly noted for her interpretations of Bach, and of Shostakovich, who was a personal friend. He wrote his 24 Preludes and Fugues for her.

ninth　The interval which consists of one octave plus a tone.

Tatiana Nikolaeva

noch *(Ger.)*   Still, yet; **noch schneller**, still faster.

nobile, nobilmente *(It.)*   Nobly, in a noble style.

nocturne *(Fr.)*, **notturno** *(It.)*   A composition which suggests the atmosphere of night. The name was popular in the 19th century as the title of short Romantic piano pieces. The Irish composer John Field invented the genre, writing 20 nocturnes, but Chopin's 19 examples are the most famous.

noel *(Fr.)*, **nowell** *(Eng.)*   A Christmas song or carol. In 17th-century France the name was given to short organ pieces based on Christmas tunes, played during Christmas services.

non *(It., Fr.)*   Not; **allegro ma non troppo**, fast, but not too fast.

notation   The way of writing down music, so that it can be played or sung: any system of notation must indicate the pitch of notes and their rhythmic values. The commonly-used Western system of a five-line staff (**staff notation**), has been in use for over 500 years; but some contemporary music uses graphic scores, in which music is indicated by patterns, and leaves the exact interpretation up to the performer.

note
    (1) A single musical sound, of fixed pitch and duration (*Amer.* **tone**)
    (2) The written symbol which represents the above.
    (3) A key (on a piano, organ or other similar instrument) which produces a pitched sound.

note-row *(Amer.* **tone-row**)   In 12-note music (see **serialism**), the order in which the composer wishes to arrange the 12 chromatic notes which make up an octave, which then forms the basic musical material of the piece.

note-values

1 semibreve (whole-note)

o

equals 2 minims (half-notes)

equals 4 crotchets (quarter-notes)

equals 8 quavers (eighth-notes)

equals 16 semiquavers (sixteenth-notes)

equals 32 demisemiquavers (thirty-second notes)

equals 64 hemidemisemiquavers (sixty-fourth notes)

notturno *(It.)*   See **nocturne**.

novelette *(Eng., Fr.)*, **Novelette** *(Ger.)*   The name given to short piano pieces of a Romantic nature, first used by Schumann for his 8 pieces, Op.21 (1838).

nuance *(Fr.)*   The word used to describe subtle variations of dynamic shading and tone colour in a musical performance.

O

obbligato *(It.)*   Essential, indispensable. The term attached to a special or unusual instrumental part which must be performed, and cannot be left out.

octave   The interval spanning 8 notes, from one note to the one above or below with the same letter name. See also **ottava**.

octet   A composition for 8 players, or the players themselves.

oeuvre *(Fr.)*   Work. Another word for a composer's output.

Ogdon, John (1937- 1989)   British pianist. Studied at the Royal Manchester College of Music, making his debut in 1959. In 1962 he took joint 1st prize with Vladimir Ashkenazy at the Tchaikovsky Competition in Moscow, which launched an international career. Huge repertoire, including many premières of contemporary works. Career curtailed by breakdown and subsequent ill-health. Married pianist Brenda Lucas, with whom he appeared in a duo partnership.

ohne *(Ger.)*   Without. Some of Beethoven's works are classified with the prefix WoO (+ number), which means 'Werke ohne Opuszahl' (work without opus number).

ondes martenot *(Fr.)*   An electronic keyboard instrument invented in the 1920s by the French musician Maurice Martenot. It has a keyboard of 5 octaves. The French composer Olivier Messaien used it in his *Turangalîla Symphony*.

op.   Abbreviation for **opus**.

open harmony   Harmony in which the notes of the chords are widely spaced.

opus, op. *(Lat.)*,   plural **opera, opp**. Work. Usually followed by a number, to indicate the numbering of a composer's works, e.g. Op.101.

ordre *(Fr.)*   A term used by 17th- and 18th-century French composers for a keyboard suite.

organ *(Ger.* **Orgel**; *Fr.* **orgue**; *It.* **organo**)   A keyboard instrument, in which air is blown through different-sized pipes to produce the sound. The various sizes of pipes are known as stops, and these control the tone-colour, from very loud to very soft. Some stops can imitate the sound of other instruments, e.g. trumpet or flute. In older organs, the flow of air is produced by hand-

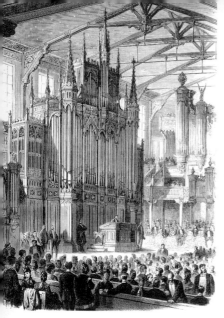

pumps, or bellows, but many modern organs work electronically. In addition to the keyboard (a large organ may have up to 6 different keyboards, known as manuals, each of which operates a different set of stops) there is usually a series of pedals, operated by the player's feet, which can be played independently, and can play a different line of music.

The organ is the oldest keyboard instrument. It was invented in Egypt in the 3rd century BC by a Greek engineer. During the later Middle Ages and early Renaissance, small portable (or **portative**) organs were popular: these had a range of about 2 octaves, and the player operated the bellows with his left hand, and played a tune with his right hand. Another type was the slightly larger **positive** organ, which stood on the floor or on a table. Large organs have always been associated with church or cathedral use, owing to their powerful, sonorous tone. The earliest kinds, dating from the 14th century, needed up to 10 people to work the bellows; but gradual improvements in design refined the mechanism, and now organists control even the largest and most powerful instruments alone.

ornaments (*Fr.* **agréments, accords**; *It.* **fioriture**; *Ger.* **Verzierungen**).
Decorations of a tune. In early vocal music, the singers were expected to improvise ornaments, but in keyboard music, they are generally indicated by special signs, such as the acciaccatura, appoggiatura, mordent, trill or shake, and turn.

ossia (*It.*)   Or else. A term used to indicate an alternative (often simplified) version of a particular musical passage, which the composer has authorized for use if necessary.

ostinato (*It.*)   'Obstinate'. A musical melodic or rhythmic phrase or motif which is repeated over and over again. **Basso ostinato**, a bass-line figure which is constantly repeated throughout the piece (see **ground bass**).

ottava (*It.*, sometimes written 8va)   Octave. An indication to play a passage an octave higher (**all'ottava**, 'at the octave'), or an octave lower (**ottava bassa**, 'low octave').

overstrung   A term used in piano building. An overstrung piano is one in which 2 sets of strings are set at different angles, one crossing over the other, to give extra length and resonance to the bass strings.

overtone   Any note of the harmonic series except the basic one, or fundamental.

P

P   Abbreviation of **pedal**.

p   Abbreviation of **piano** *(It.)*, soft.

pp   Abbreviation of **pianissimo** *(It.)*, very soft, often mysterious.

ppp   Even softer than **pianissimo**. Beethoven used this term only once, in the 3rd movement of his Piano Sonata no.4 in E flat major, Op.7.

Pachelbel, Johann (1653 1706)   German organist and composer, an important precursor of J.S. Bach. His most famous composition is the Canon for 3 violins and continuo, but his keyboard music includes 78 chorale preludes and several sets of variations for harpsichord, including *Hexachordum Apollinis* (1699).

Pachmann, Vladimir (1848-1933)   Russian pianist. He studied at the Vienna Conservatory, and made his début in 1869. After further study he resumed his concert career at the age of 34, touring Britain and the USA with great success. He was particularly associated with the music of Chopin.

Paderewski, Ignacy Jan (1860-1941)   Polish pianist and composer. A famous international concert pianist, he became closely involved with the cause of Polish nationalism, and after the First World War, he was briefly Prime Minister of Poland. His piano works include a Concerto, the *Polish Fantasy* for piano and orchestra, a Sonata, a set of Variations, *6 Concert Humoresques* (of which no.1 is the famous Minuet in G), and many shorter pieces, including the *Tatra Album* (1885).

A cartoon of Paderewski

Paganini Variations   Several composers, including Brahms (*Variations on a Theme of Paganini* for piano), Rakhmaninov (*Rhapsody on a Theme of Paganini* for piano and orchestra) and Lutoslawski (*Variations on a Theme of Paganini* for 2 pianos) have written variations on the famous theme from Paganini's 24th Caprice in A minor. Schumann's 12 *Études de concert* (1832-3) are also based on Paganini's caprices, as are Liszt's 6 *Études d'exécution transcendante d'après Paganini*.

Papillons *(Fr.)*   Butterflies. The title of 12 short piano pieces by Schumann, Op.2 (1829-31).

parallel motion   See **motion**.

Paraphrases

(1) A collection of piano duets based on *Chopsticks*, by various composers including Liszt, Borodin and Rimsky-Korsakov.

(2) Liszt's sets of variations on popular operatic tunes of the time are known as *Paraphrases*.

parlando, parlate *(It.)*   In a speaking style.

part

(1) The individual line of music performed by a single instrument or voice.

(2) The actual piece of music used by a performer in an ensemble.

parte *(It.)*   Part. See also under **colla**.

Parthenia   The title given to the first book of keyboard music printed in England (1611). It contained 21 pieces by Byrd, Bull and Gibbons.

partita *(It.)*

(1) A variation.

(2) The name sometimes given (wrongly) to a suite, e.g. the 6 Partitas in J.S. Bach's *Klavierübung* (1731).

passacaglia *(It.)*; **passacaille** *(Fr.)*   A composition built over a ground bass, originally a triple-time dance. Identical to **chaconne**.

passage   A small section of a larger composition.

passage-work   The name given to brilliant figuration played by a soloist, often a pianist.

passepied *(Fr.)*   A lively dance, often in running quavers or semiquavers, in 3/8 or 6/8 time. It was related to the minuet, and was originally performed as a court dance in Brittany. During the late 17th century it was introduced to the court of Louis XIV. Debussy wrote a *Passepied* (in duple time) in his *Suite bergamasque*.

The title-page of 'Parthenia'

passing note   A note which does not belong to the chord with which it is heard, but is used to lead melodically from one consonance to another.

pasticcio *(It.)* 'Pie'. A composition containing sections by different composers, such as the *Hexameron* (1837).

pastiche *(Fr.)* Imitation. A piece written by one composer in the style of another.

pastorale *(It.)* A piece which suggests a rural scene. In the Baroque era, 'pastoral' music was usually in compound time, and often in F major.

'Pastoral' Sonata The nickname given to Beethoven's Piano Sonata in D major, Op.28 (1801).

'Pathétique' Sonata (Pathetic Sonata) Beethoven's own name (*Grande sonate pathétique*) for his piano sonata no.8 in C minor, Op.13 (1798-9).

pause *(Eng; Ger.)*; **point d'orgue** *(Fr.)*; **fermata** *(It.)* The sign ⌒ which, when placed over a note, indicates that it should be held for longer than usual. The performer must decide how long. If the sign appears over a bar line, it indicates a short silence.

pavan *(Eng.)*, **pavane** *(Fr.)*, **pavana** *(It.)* An Italian dance popular in the 16th and 17th centuries, which may have come from the area round Padua. It is in simple duple time, with a dignified, courtly character. It was usually followed by the faster and livelier galliard. Some later composers have used the name and style, such as Ravel's *Pavane pour une infante défunte* (Pavan for a dead Infanta) for piano.

Ped. Abbrevation for pedal.

Piano pedals

pedal
    (1) A lever operated by the foot, and found on pianos, harpsichords, organs, harps and timpani.
    (2) In piano music, the sign **Ped.** or **ped.** means depress the sustaining pedal with the right foot, and keep it down until told to release it. In organ music, it means play with the feet (on the pedal-board).
    (3) In harmony, a **pedal note** or **pedal point** is a note (usually in the bass) which is sustained while harmonies change above it.
    (4) The lowest note of a harmonic series.

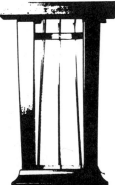

pedal board A keyboard played with the feet, usually found on organs, but sometimes also on other keyboard instruments.

pedal-piano A piano which has a pedal board as well as a keyboard, sometimes used by organists for practising at home.

pedal point   See **pedal** (3).

pentatonic scale   A scale of 5 different notes, found by playing the five black keys of the piano, generally starting on F sharp. It is used in folk music all over the world, and by composers such as Debussy and Bartók.

Perahia, Murray (b.1947)   American pianist. He studied at Mannes College, making his début in New York in 1972. In that year he won the Leeds International Piano Competition, which launched

Murray Perahia

his international career. One of the most sensitive and intelligent pianists of his generation, he specializes in Mozart, Beethoven, Chopin and Schumann.

perdendo, perdendosi *(It.)*   Dying away. Play softer and softer until the sound disappears.

perfect cadence   See **cadence**.

perfect intervals   See **interval**.

perfect pitch (absolute pitch)   Someone who can sing any note absolutely in tune without having heard it first (i.e. by storing the pitch in their memory) is said to have 'perfect pitch'. **'Relative pitch'** is the ability to sing notes in tune having previously heard a single note.

perfect time   See **common time**.

perpetual motion *(Lat.* **perpetuum mobile**; *It.* **moto perpetuo**; *Fr.* **mouvement perpetuel**)   See **moto**.

pesante *(It.)*   Heavily.

Petri, Egon (1881-1962)   German pianist, a pupil of Teresa Carreño from the age of 3, and a friend and disciple of Busoni. He made his début in 1902, and later taught in Manchester, Basle and Berlin. In 1940, after a successful career as a touring virtuoso, he settled in the USA, teaching and continuing to give recitals up to the age of 79. His repertoire ranged from Bach to Busoni.

peu à peu *(Fr.)*   Little by little, gradually.

pezzo *(It.)*   Piece.

Phantasie *(Ger.)*   Fantasy; **Phantasiestück**, 'fantasy piece' (see **Fantasiestück**).

phrase   A short section of a piece, often covered by a curved line. The phrases which make up a melody or a whole piece tend to be natural divisions, such as could be sung in one breath. Each is like a spoken sentence, with punctuation – musical commas and full-stops. Each phrase normally moves towards a natural climax. A melody of 16 bars will often divide up naturally into four phrases, each of four bars; but longer and shorter divisions are quite common.

phrasing   The art of emphasizing the natural divisions or phrases of a piece or melody, to reveal its structure to an audience.

phrase-mark   The curved line which indicates a phrase. It will always cover more than 2 notes, and must not be confused with either a couplet or a tie, which link two notes only.

piacere *(It.)*   Pleasure; **a piacere**, at the performer's discretion, i.e. play freely.

piacevole *(It.)*   Pleasantly.

piangendo, piangente *(It.)*   Weeping; **piangevole**, plaintively.

pianissimo *(It.*, abbreviated to *pp* or *ppp*)   Very soft, often mysteriously.

piano *(It.)*
 (1) Soft, i.e. an instruction to the performer to play quietly. Abbreviated to *p*.
 (2) Abbreviation for **pianoforte**. This keyboard instrument was invented by Bartolomeo Cristofori at the beginning of the 18th century in Florence. Unlike the harpsichord, which lacked dynamic range since its strings were plucked, the piano had a set of hammers which hit the strings – either hard (producing a loud tone) or more gently (producing a soft tone) according to how the player touched the keys. The earliest pianos were wing-shaped like harpsichords, and had horizontal strings: by the mid-18th century, makers had developed the square (actually rectangular) piano; while makers such as the Englishman John Broadwood, the Frenchman Érard and the Austrian Andreas Stein – whose instruments were favoured by Mozart – eventually settled on the grand piano shape which we know today. Grand pianos now come in several sizes, including a full-sized, or 'concert' grand, measuring 9 feet in length; a medium size, or 'boudoir' grand, measuring around 6 feet; and a small 'baby' grand, suitable for use in the home. Around 1800 an American maker called John Hawkins invented an upright piano, in which the strings are perpendicular: this type became very popular for home use where space was limited. Hawkins also replace the original wooden frame by a much stronger iron one, able to take thicker, tighter strings, which gave the instrument more depth of tone.
 From around 1835, some pianos were 'overstrung', i.e. they had two sets of strings of graduated thicknesses, crossing one another. Unlike harpsichords, which had only one string to a note, pianos have always had at least 2: a modern piano has one very thick string to each of its very lowest notes; 2 for notes in the middle register, and 3 for the highest notes. Below the strings (on a grand) or behind them (on an upright) is a wooden board called the

The interior of an upright piano, showing frame, soundboard and strings

Piano action

An early 19th-century upright piano

A late 19th-century upright piano

The first Steinway piano, made in Germany in 1836

The elaborate Steinway grand built for the 1876 Centennial Exhibition in Philadelphia

sound-board, which amplifies the tone. The hammers are made of wood, covered with felt: when the key is pressed down, the hammer hits the string and makes it vibrate. The hammer then bounces back and is caught by an 'escapement', which prevents it from hitting the string again. When the player releases the key, a soft pad called a damper comes into contact with the string and stops it from ringing on.

A modern Broadwood grand

Modern pianos have at least 2, and sometimes 3, pedals: the one on the right is the sustaining pedal, which, when depressed, removes all the dampers from the strings, allowing the sound to continue to resonate, even if the fingers are taken away from the keys. The left pedal (sometimes called the 'soft' or 'damping' pedal), lessens the sound, either by moving the keyboard sideways (only on grand pianos), which allows the hammers to strike only one string per note, or (on upright pianos) by moving the hammers nearer to the strings, so they have a shorter distance to travel (which also reduces the sound). Some pianos have a middle pedal, called the sostenuto pedal, which allows the player to select certain notes to be sustained, without affecting others.

Pianos are used in a variety of ways: as a solo instrument; as the most common accompaniment to a string, woodwind or brass instrument; as a concerto instrument, or in chamber music. In the 20th century, composers such as Bartók and Stravinsky have also used the piano as an orchestral instrument, usually allied to the percussion department.

piano duet   2 performers on one piano, or the music written for them, such as Debussy's *Petite Suite*, or Ravel's *Ma mère l'oye* (Mother Goose); or 2 performers at separate pianos - such as the celebrated Labèque sisters - or the music written for them.

piano quartet   A chamber music combination consisting of piano, violin, viola and cello – or the music written for them.

piano quintet   A chamber music combination consisting normally of piano plus string quartet, or the music written for them; but Schubert's famous *Trout* Quintet is scored for piano, violin, viola, cello and double bass.

piano trio   A chamber music combination consisting of piano, violin and cello, or the music written for them. Haydn, Mozart, Beethoven and Brahms wrote famous piano trios.

pianoforte *(It.)* 'Soft-loud'. See **piano** (2).

pianola   One type of 'player-piano'. These are mechanical pianos, in which the keys work by air-pressure, supplied by bellows, or by electricity. The air is blown through holes on a paper roll, which unwinds as the piece progresses. Sometimes the rolls could reproduce performances by famous pianists, so it is possible to hear how Debussy or Rakhmaninov for instance, would have played certain pieces of their own music. Stravinsky wrote an *Étude* for pianola, and transcribed many of his orchestral works for the instrument.

pitch   The exact height or depth of a note in the scale. It depends on the number of vibrations produced by the instrument or voice: fast vibrations produce a high note, and slow ones a low note. Pitch has varied considerably over the centuries, and in 'authentic' modern performances of Renaissance, Baroque and Classical music, musicians tune to what would have been the pitch of the day. Modern 'concert pitch', however, to which pianos and orchestras are now routinely tuned, is determined by the note A above middle C, which should vibrate 440 times per second. Pitch is measured either by a tuning fork, or by an electronically produced signal.

più *(It.)*   More; **più lento**, more slowly; **più mosso**, more movement, quicker; **più tosto**, rather quicker.

pizzicato *(It.)*   Plucked.

plagal cadence   See **cadence**.

player-piano   See **pianola**.

plectrum   A small piece of bone, wood, ivory, etc., which is used to pluck the strings of certain instruments, including the harpsichord.

Pleyel, Ignaz (1757-1831)   Austrian composer, pianist and piano manufacturer. He studied with Haydn and eventually settled in Paris, where he became a music dealer and opened a piano factory. Piano works include 2 concertos, around 50 piano trios, 4 sonatas, a piano method including 27 exercises, and other pieces.

poco *(It.)*   A little; **poco più mosso**, a little more movement; **poco lento**, rather slowly; **poco à poco**, little by little; **pochetto**, very little; **pochissimo**, the least possible.

Pogorelich, Ivo (b.1958)   Croatian pianist. Studied in Moscow, winning the 1980 Montreal International Competition. His sensational elimination the same year in the International Chopin Competition caused a furore, leading to massive publicity and worldwide exposure.

poi *(It.)*   Then; **poi la coda**, then on to the coda.

point d'orgue *(Fr.)*   Organ point.
(1) see **pedal**.
(2) The pause sign.
(3) A cadenza in a concerto.

polka   A Bohemian dance in quick duple time. Invented in the early 19th century, it soon became all the rage in ballrooms all over Europe.

Pollini, Maurizio (b.1942)   Italian pianist, a pupil of Michelangeli. In 1960 he won first prize in the International Chopin Competition. A pianist of formidable technique and intellect, his repertoire ranges from the classics to contemporary music.

Maurizio Pollini

polonaise *(Fr.)*, **Polonase** *(Ger.)*, **polacca**
(It.)   An aristocratic Polish dance in triple time, dating from the 16th century. Regarded as representing the true national spirit of Poland, it nevertheless became especially popular in Germany and Scandinavia. Many composers, including Bach, Handel, Mozart, Beethoven, Schubert, Schumann and Liszt wrote polonaises (Bach included a polonaise in his 6th *French Suite*) – but Chopin's 13 piano polonaises – regarded as the supreme musical symbol of Polish nationalism – are the most famous examples.

polyphony *(Gr.)*   'Many sounds'. A term used to describe music in which several independent strands (melodic lines, or 'voices') combine to weave a texture. Polyphony has virtually the same meaning as counterpoint, though a vocal composition is more likely to be described as **polyphonic**, and an instrumental one as **contrapuntal**. See also **homophony**.

polyrhythm   A rhythmic texture created by different rhythms being performed simultaneously.

polytonality   Music in which several different keys are heard together.

pomposo *(It.)*   Majestic, pompous.

portamento *(It.)*   Joining notes very smoothly together.

postlude   A piece played at the end.

Poulenc, Francis (1899-1963)   French composer and pianist, one of the group of early 20th-century French composers known as 'Les Six'. Keyboard works include *Concert champêtre* for harpsichord or piano; *Aubade*, a concerto for piano and 18 instruments; Concerto for 2 pianos and orchestra;

Concerto for piano and orchestra; Concerto for organ, strings and timpani; solo piano pieces including *6 Impromptus*; 10 *Promenades*; *Napoli Suite*; *Pastourelle*; *2 Nouvelettes*; *8 Nocturnes*; 12 *Improvisations*; *Suite française*; *Les soirées de Nazelles*; Intermezzo in A flat; *Improvisation* in D; *Hommage à Edith Piaf*; Sonata for piano duet; for 2 pianos: Sonata; *Élégie*.

pp, ppp   Abbreviations for **pianissimo**, very soft.

Praeludium *(Ger.)*   Prelude.

Pralltriller *(Ger.)*   Upper mordent.

préambule *(Fr.)*   Prelude.

precipitato, precipitando, precipitoso *(It.)*   Impetuously.

preciso *(It.)*   Precise, exact.

pre-classical   Music written in the period immediately before Haydn and Mozart, by composers such as C.P.E. Bach.

prelude
(1) A piece of music played at the beginning of a work such as an opera.
(2) A short keyboard piece, often coupled with a fugue, such as Bach's 48 preludes and fugues which make up the collection known as *The Well-Tempered Clavier*.
(3) A short, independent keyboard piece. Chopin's 25, Rakhmaninov's 13 and Debussy's 24 are among the most famous examples.

prepared piano   A piano whose strings have been tampered with, to produce different sounds – for example, by inserting pieces of wood or material at various places along the string. Composers such as John Cage have made much use of prepared pianos.

pressez *(Fr.)*   Get faster.

presto *(It.)*   Very fast; **prestissimo**, as fast as possible.

primo, prima *(It.)*   First. The top part in piano duets, as opposed to *secondo*, the lower part. **Tempo primo**, return to the original speed; **come prima**, as at first; **prima volta**, first time.

programme music   Music that tells a story, or tries to depict an event or a landscape. It may sometimes be based on literature, e.g. Liszt's *Dante* Sonata.

progression   A meaningful sequence of notes or chords which lead towards a goal, such as a cadence.

Prokofiev, Sergey (1891-1953)   Russian composer and pianist. After beginning a promising career as a composer, he left Russia in 1918 after the Revolution and settled in the USA. From 1920 to 1933 he lived in Paris, before

Sergey Prokofiev aged 10

returning to the Soviet Union. His last years were overshadowed by criticism from Stalin. Piano works include 5 concertos; 10 sonatas; 2 sonatinas; *4 Études*; 18 *Pieces* (published in 3 volumes); *Sarcasms*; *Visions fugitives*; *Grandmother's Tales*.

Pugno, Raoul (1852-1914)   French pianist. Studied at the Paris Conservatoire, where he later taught. Champion of contemporary French music by Debussy, Saint-Saëns and Ravel, also editor of Chopin complete piano works.

pulse   See **beat**.

Purcell, Henry (1659-1695)   English composer and organist. A pupil of John Blow, he became composer to the royal band of violins, and in 1679, organist of Westminster Abbey. Three years later, he was appointed organist of the Chapel Royal. His early death robbed English music of one of its finest composers. Harpsichord music includes 8 suites, *Musick's Handmaid*, and assorted individual pieces including a Hornpipe, a Toccata and 2 Pavans.

Q

Quadrat *(Ger.)* The natural sign ♮.

quadrille A type of dance popular at the French court of the Emperor Napoleon Bonaparte. It was danced in a square formation. The music consisted of a mixture of popular tunes, airs from operas, and so on.

quadruple time A time-signature in which there are four beats to the bar, e.g. 4/4.

quadruplet A group of four notes of equal value, played in the time of three.

quarter note The American term for the crotchet.

quarter-tone An interval half the size of a semitone. It cannot be played on a piano, but other instruments, especially strings, can play quarter-tones easily. In the 20th century, special pianos capable of playing quarter-tones have been built, and composers such as Alois Hába have written music for them.

quartet *(Eng.)*, **quatuor** *(Fr.)*, **Quartett** *(Ger.)*, **quartetto** *(It.)* A composition for four players or voices, or the group which performs such music. A piano quartet usually consists of piano, violin, viola and cello, but Messiaen's *Quatuor pour le fin du temps* (Quartet for the end of time) is scored for piano, clarinet, violin and cello.

quasi *(It.)* As if, almost. Beethoven's title for his Moonlight Sonata – Sonata quasi una fantasia – means 'sonata in the style of a fantasia'.

quaver (*Fr.* **croche**; *Ger.* **Achtelnote**; *It.* **croma**; *Amer.* **eighth-note**) The note which is half a crotchet in length. It is written ♪ and its corresponding rest is written 𝄾 .

quintet A composition for 5 performers or voices, or the music written for such a group. A piano quintet normally consists of piano and string quartet.

quintuple time A time-signature in which there are 5 units in the bar, e.g. 5/4, 5/8.

quintuplet A group of 5 notes played in the time of 3 or 4.

quodlibet *(Lat.)* 'What you please'. A composition in which fragments of popular tunes are mixed up together, usually as a joke. The finale of Bach's *Goldberg Variations* for harpsichord is a quodlibet.

R

R. Abbreviation for right, as in **R.H.**, right hand.

ragtime An early type of jazz, especially for solo piano, which used to be played in cafes and bars in the American Deep South from about 1895 to 1920. It is characterized by a syncopated, or 'ragged' rhythm. The most famous ragtime composer was Scott Joplin, whose rag *The Entertainer* was used as the theme music for the film *The Sting*.

'Raindrop' Prelude The nickname for Chopin's Piano Prelude in D flat major, Op.28 no.15 (1839), written while he was staying in Majorca. The persistent repeated note A flat is said to have been suggested by the dripping of rain on the roof of his lodgings.

Rakhmaninov, Sergey (1873-1943) Russian composer and pianist. He wrote his 1st Piano Concerto at 18, and the famous Prelude in C sharp minor a year later. His popular 2nd Piano Concerto, written in 1900, was a great success at its first performance. After working at the Bolshoy Theatre in Moscow, Rakhmaninov moved to Dresden in 1906: 3 years later he visited the USA, where he gave the first performance of his 3rd Piano Concerto. In 1917 he left Russia permanently for America, where he earned his living as a concert pianist. One of the greatest of all pianists, he also wrote a 4th Concerto; the ever-popular *Rhapsody on a theme of Paganini* for piano and orchestra; 3 Nocturnes; 4 Pieces; 5 *Morceaux de fantasie*; 7 *Morceaux de salon*; 6 *Moments musicaux*; 23 Preludes; 15 *Études tableaux*; 2 sonatas; *Oriental Sketch*; and *Variations on a theme of Corelli*.

The title page of a piano rag, 1905

Sergey Rakhmaninov

rallentando, rall. *(It.)*   Gradually getting slower.

Rameau, Jean-Philippe (1683-1764)   French composer, harpsichordist and organist. He began his career as organist in various French cities, before settling in Paris, where he taught harpsichord, and published an important treatise on harmony. Although he was best-known as an opera composer, Rameau's harpsichord works, published in 3 books of suites, are among the most important 18th-century works for the instrument.

rapsodie *(Fr.)*   See **rhapsody**.

Rasch *(Ger.)*   Quickly.

Ravel, Maurice (1875-1937)   French composer and pianist. He studied with Fauré at the Paris Conservatoire, and became one of the most important composers of piano literature of his time, rivalling Debussy. His piano works include a Concerto in G; a Concerto for the left hand (written for the one-armed pianist Paul Wittgenstein); *Sérénade grotesque*; *Menuet antique*; *Pavane pour une infante défunte*; *Jeux d'eau*; *Sonatine*; *Miroirs*; *Gaspard de la nuit*; *Menuet sur le nom d'Haydn*; *Valses nobles et sentimentales*; *À la manière de (1) Borodin (2) Chabrier*; *Le tombeau de Couperin*; *Ma mère l'oye* for piano duet; and, for 2 pianos, *Sites auriculaires* and *Frontispice*, the latter for 5 hands!

realization   The filling out – by the performer – of music left by its composer in a sketchy or incomplete form, such as figured bass.

Maurice Ravel

An extract from the autograph of Ravel's 'Jeux d'eau'

recapitulation   A section of a piece in which the original themes, presented at the beginning of the exposition, return more or less complete shortly before the end.

recital   A musical performance by one or 2 performers, playing solo works, sonatas, etc. It was originally only applied to singers, but Liszt was the first pianist to be described as giving a recital.

reel   A fast-moving dance from Scotland, Ireland or northern England, usually in 4/4 time, with continuous melodic movement. The Highland fling is a Scottish example.

Reger, Max (1873-1916)   German pianist, composer and organist. He taught at the conservatories in Munich and Leipzig, while also giving concert tours. His enormous output for keyboard includes 4 sonatinas and many shorter works for piano; 2 suites, 2 sonatas, choral fantasias, preludes and fugues, and many shorter works for organ.

register
(1) A set of organ pipes belonging to one particular stop.
(2) A certain part of the range of an instrument or voice, e.g. its high or low register.

Reinecke, Carl (1824-1910)   German pianist, composer, conductor and teacher He eventually settled in Leipzig, where he conducted the famous Gewandhaus orchestra, and taught piano and composition at the Conservatory. His piano works include 4 concertos, sonatas, sonatinas, and many smaller pieces for pupils and young players.

relative (major, minor)   A term used to describe the relationship between a major and a minor key which share the same key signature, e.g. F minor is the relative minor of D major (both keys have one flat in the signature), and D major is the relative major of F minor. The relative minor of a major key is found by counting a minor 3rd down from the major key-note.

relative pitch   Someone who can relate the pitch of other notes to one given note is said to have 'relative pitch'. See **perfect pitch**.

repeat marks   If a section of music is to be repeated, several signs are used to save the composer writing the same music over again. The symbol :‖ means go back to ‖: , or else to the beginning of the piece. The letters D.C. (*da capo*) mean go back to the beginning; while the letters D.S. (*dal segno*, 'from the sign') mean go back to the mark 𝄋 . *D.C. al Segno e poi la Coda* means 'return to the beginning, play through until you reach the sign 𝄋 and then go straight to the Coda'. In French music, *bis* means play the passage twice.
Sometimes, when a section is repeated, it needs 2 different endings, the first suitable for returning to the beginning, and the second suitable for

leading on to the next section. In this case, first (second) time bars are used.

Musical shorthand is also used for repeated notes:

reprise *(Fr.)*   Repeat, especially meaning a return to the first section after a contrasting section.

resolution   The term used to describe a discordant chord followed by a harmonious one (a concord) – the discord is said to have 'resolved'.

resonance

(1) The sympathetic vibrations set up in a sound-producing body by the sounding of a note similar in pitch to the fundamental of that object (see **harmonics**), or one of its overtones.

(2) A 'resonant' acoustic is one in which sound-waves bounce back off the walls, amplifying and continuing the sound, rather than being absorbed by soft materials such as curtains, which create a 'dry' acoustic.

rest

(1) A silence in music.

(2) The symbols used to notate silences of various durations. These include the following:

semibreve   minim   crotchet   quaver   semiquaver   demisemiquaver

The semibreve or whole-note rest is used to indicate a whole bar's rest in any time-signature. If several consecutive bars are silent, the rest is often indicated thus:

Rests can be dotted to increase their value by half, in the same way as notes.

restez *(Fr.)*   Stay. Linger on a note, rather than hurrying off it.

retenant, retenu *(Fr.)*   Holding back, held back. Same as **ritenuto**.

Reubke, Julius (1834-1858)   German pianist and composer, a pupil of Liszt. Keyboard music includes an Organ Sonata on Psalm 94, a Piano Sonata, and solo works for piano.

rhapsody   A single-movement composition, often of a Romantic, fanciful type. Rakhmaninov's *Rhapsody on a Theme of Paganini* (1934) for piano and orchestra consists of 24 variations on Paganini's famous A minor Caprice for solo violin. Gershwin's *Rhapsody in Blue* for piano and orchestra was inspired by jazz.

rhythm   The element of music which deals with time, or duration, as opposed to pitch. Most music is divided up into regular cells, or beats, combined into groups of 2, 3, 4, etc., and divided visually by means of bar lines. These units can then be combined into larger phrases, by means of accentuation. In 20th-century music, composers have experimented with freer rhythms, including unusual or constantly changing time-signatures, polyrhythm (in which several different rhythms are combined simultaneously), and even indeterminancy, in which performers decide the duration, tempo and order of performance of individual notes, phrases, or sections.

ricercar, ricercare *(It.)*   Research. To seek out: a term applied in Baroque music to certain types of contrapuntal instrumental pieces in fugal style, such as Bach's pieces in his *Musical Offering*, or to contrapuntal preludes.

Richter, Sviatoslav (b.1914)   Russian pianist, a pupil of Heinrich Neuhaus at the Moscow Conservatory. One of the finest pianists of his generation, he made his British and American débuts in the early 1960s, and now makes occasional public appearances in the West. Repertoire encompasses the classics and romantics, through to Prokofiev and Shostakovich.

Sviatoslav Richter

ridicoloso *(It.)*   Preposterous, absurd. A term used occasionally by Prokofiev.

rigaudon *(Fr.)*, **rigadoon** *(Eng.)*   A Provençal folkdance, later taken up with enthusiasm by the French court of Louis XIV, which quickly became equally popular in England and Germany. The court version was a lively dance in duple or quadruple time, usually starting with an upbeat, and involving a particular group of steps (hop, step, step, jump). Purcell, Pachelbel, François Couperin and Rameau, among others, wrote rigaudons for keyboard, and the dance was adopted in the 18th century as an optional movement in the Baroque suite. It reappeared later in works such as MacDowell's *Air et rigaudon* for piano, Op.49 No.2, and in Ravel's *Le tombeau de Couperin*.

rinforzando, rinforzato *(It.,* abbreviated to *rf* or *rfz)* Reinforcing, reinforced. Stressed, accented.

risoluto *(It.)* Resolute.

ritardando, ritard., rit. *(It.)* Gradually slowing down.

ritenuto *(It.)* Held back (immediately, not gradually, like *ritardando*).

ritmico *(It.)* Rhythmic.

rock A type of pop music, originally called **rock'n'roll**, which began in the USA in the 1950s. There are now several offshoots, such as punk rock.

rococo A term applied to the decorative, delicately ornamental style of music written in the mid 18th-century, by composers such as C.P.E. Bach and Haydn.

romance *(Eng., Fr.)*, **Romanze** *(Ger.)*, **romanza** *(It.)* A name sometimes given to any piece of music of a tender, reflective kind. Schumann wrote 3 *Romanzen* for piano; while Mozart called the slow movement of his D minor Piano Concerto, K466, a 'Romance'.

romanesca *(It.)*
    (1) An old Italian dance.
    (2) An Italian melody often used in the 17th century as a ground bass.

Romanticism The term first used to describe a type of literature written in the late 18th and early 19th centuries, dealing with subjects such as love, nature and death, and applied to music written between around 1830 and 1900. Music described as 'Romantic' can express an emotional state, depict a landscape, or tell a story. Many composers of Romantic music, such as Berlioz, Liszt, Schubert, Schumann and Weber, were greatly influenced by literature (e.g. Schumann's *Kreisleriana* for piano), but others such as Chopin and Brahms were inspired by less obvious models.

rondo *(It.)*, **rondeau** *(Fr.)* Round. A musical composition in which one section keeps repeating, usually with contrasting sections in between, resulting in an ABACADA (etc.) structure. In the Classical period, the rondo was a favourite form for the last movements of sonatas or concertos. Mozart wrote several independent rondos for piano, such as the Rondo in A minor, K.511.

root The note on which a chord is built, the lowest note if it is in its basic position (known as **root position**). In the common chord of C major (C-E-G), the root is C.

Rosenthal, Moritz (1862-1946) Polish pianist, a pupil of Liszt. After studies in Vienna he began a concert career, making his American début in 1888. In 1912 he became pianist to the Viennese court. His repertoire ranged from Scarlatti to Debussy, but he was especially famed for his Chopin recitals.

Rossini, Gioacchino (1792-1868)   Italian composer of operas (including *The Barber of Seville*), who 'retired' from the stage at the early age of 37, having made his fortune. In later life he wrote several delightful short pieces, including some for piano.

round   A short, unaccompanied vocal canon, such as *London's Burning*, in which the voices enter in turn.

Roussel, Albert (1869-1937)   French composer, a pupil of d'Indy. Best known for his orchestral music. Piano works include *Rustiques* (1904-6), Suite (1909-10); *Sonatine* (1912); *3 Pièces* (1933).

row   See **note-row**.

Rubato *(It.)*   'Robbed'. A type of performance in which the player does not always keep absolutely strict time, but adopts a flexible approach in which some phrases or passages are played quicker, and others slower – i.e. 'stealing' time from some places and 'paying it back' later. The music of Schumann and Chopin requires much *rubato*.

Rubinstein, Anton (1829-1894)   Russian pianist and composer. He studied in Germany, but then returned to St Petersburg, where he founded the Conservatory in 1862. One of the greatest pianists of his time, he wrote a great deal of music including 20 operas and 5 piano concertos, but is chiefly remembered for his *Melody in F* for piano.

A cartoon of Anton Rubinstein on his London visit, 1886

Rubinstein, Artur (1887-1982)   Polish pianist, one of the greatest virtuosi of all time. After early wanderings he finally settled in the USA in 1939. His mastery of the classics, Chopin and contemporary works by Falla, Szymanowski and Villa-Lobos, among others, was unrivalled. Had duo partnership with violinist Ysaÿe. He was still playing up to the age of 90.

Ruggles, Carl (1876-1971)   American composer, one of the most important of the 20th century. His piano works include *Polyphonic Composition* for 3 pianos (1940) and *Evocations* (1937-44).

ruhig *(Ger.)*   Calmly.

rumba   A Cuban dance in 8/8 time, which was taken up in jazz around 1930. Arthur Benjamin wrote a *Jamaican Rumba* for piano.

Rustle of Spring   A piano piece (no.3 of Op.32, 1909) by the Norwegian composer Christian Sinding.

Artur Rubinstein

Camille Saint-Saëns, aged 10

S

S *(Ger.)*　The note E flat.

Saint-Saëns, Camille (1835-1921)　F r e n c h pianist and composer. A highly talented child prodigy, he entered the Paris Conservatoire at 13, and later became organist at several Paris churches, and co-founder of the Société National de Musique. His piano works include 5 concertos, 6 Bagatelles, 2 sets of Études; 6 Fugues, and several works for 2 pianos including *Caprice arabe* and *Caprice héroïque*.

saltarello *(It.)*　A lively Italian dance, often in 6/8 time.

samba　An Afro-Brazilian dance, popular around Rio de Janeiro from the 1920s onwards.

sans *(Fr.)*　Without.

saraband *(Eng.)*, **sarabande** *(Fr.)*　A Baroque dance in triple time, originating in Spain or Latin America, which became part of the standard Baroque suite, coming after the courante and before the final gigue. It was normally slow and stately, in character (although the Italians, Spaniards and English preferred a faster version), and in the 17th century it acquired the characteristic rhythmic pattern in which the second beat is accented. The sarabande was particularly popular with French composers such as François Couperin and Rameau, and with Germans including Handel, J.S. and J.C. Bach. Debussy resurrected the form in his suite *Pour le piano* (1896-1901), and in the first book of *Images* (1905).

Satie, Erik (1866-1925)　French composer. After early studies at the Paris Conservatoire, he earned his living as a pianist in Parisian bars and cabarets. In 1905 he 'went back to school', studying composition with d'Indy and Roussel, and in later life became a cult figure among younger composers. His eccentric compositions, deliberately written in a sparse, archaic style, and with amusing 'nonsense' titles and instructions, include the popular *3 Gymnopédies* (1888); *3 Gnossiennes*, 1890; *2 Pièces froides* (Cold pieces, 1897); 3

Erik Satie in 1924,
by Francis Picabia

Nouvelles pièces froides (New cold pieces); *3 morceaux en forme de poire* (Pear-shaped pieces, 1903), *Aperçus désagreables* (Disagreeable glances, 1908-12), *En habit de cheval* (Dressed as a horse, 1911), all for piano duet; *3 véritables preludes flasques (pour un chien)* (Really flabby preludes (for a dog), 1912); 3 *Embryons desséchés* (Dried-up embryos, 1913); 3 *Croquis et agaceries d'un gros bonhomme en bois* (Sketches and irritations of a great big fat wooden man, 1913); 3 *Chapitres tournés en tous sens* (Chapters turned all ways, 1913); *Enfantines* (Childishnesses, 1913); *Sports et divertissements* (Sports and recreations, 1914); *Heures séculaires et instantanées* (Secular and instantaneous hours, 1914); *Avant-dernières pensées* (Next-to-last thoughts, 1915); *Sonatine bureaucratique* (Bureaucratic sonatina, 1917); *5 nocturnes* (1919)

scale *(Eng.)*, **scala** *(It.)*, **Tonleiter** *(Ger.)*, **gamme** *(Fr.)*   A series of notes progressing upwards or downwards by step. Our major and minor scales, each with 8 notes to the octave, developed from the old modes, and are known as **diatonic scales**, as opposed to **chromatic scales**, which progress by semitones. Similar to the chromatic scale is the **dodecaphonic scale**, which consists of 12 equal notes, without a key-note. The **whole-tone scale**, consisting of 6 notes to the octave, has no semitones, and can only be found in two positions:

while the **pentatonic scale** has only 5 different notes, and is often found in Far Eastern music. It can be imitated by playing only the black keys of the piano:

Scarlatti, Domenico (1685-1757)   Italian composer and harpsichordist, son of the famous opera composer Alessandro Scarlatti (1660-1725). In 1721 he became court harpsichordist to the King of Portugal and teacher of Princess

Domenico Scarlatti

Maria Barbara; later, when the princess married the Spanish Crown Prince in 1729, Scarlatti went with her to Madrid, where he stayed until 1754. His one-movement harpsichord sonatas, around 550 of them, are most unusual: they have a strong Spanish flavour, and introduce many important technical devices and forms taken up by later keyboard composers.

scherzando, scherzoso *(It.)* Playfully.

scherzetto, scherzino *(It.)* A little scherzo.

scherzo *(It.)* A joke. A term, first applied to vocal music, but later to instrumental works, which implied a fast, light-hearted movement. In the late 18th century, the scherzo began to replace the older, more formal minuet and trio as the 3rd (sometimes the 2nd) movement of a larger piece, such as a symphony, string quartet or sonata. Some scherzos have trio sections. In the 19th century, scherzos were sometimes composed as independent pieces. Chopin wrote 4 for piano.

Schiff, András (b.1953) Hungarian pianist. Studied at the Ferenc Liszt Academy in Budapest, where he made his début. Prizewinner at the 1974 Tchaikovsky and 1975 Leeds International Competitions. Famed for his idiosyncratic Bach interpretations.

Schlussel *(Ger.)* Clef.

Schnabel, Artur (1881-1949) Austrian pianist, a pupil of Leschetitzky, and one of the greatest 20th-century performers. He met Brahms at 12, and made his début in Vienna at 16. For many years he worked in Berlin, until the Nazi threat drove him to the USA. After the war he returned to Europe. In 1931 he became the first pianist to record all the Beethoven piano works. After starting out with a wide-ranging repertoire, he ended as a Mozart, Schubert, Beethoven and Brahms specialist. He died in Switzerland.

András Schiff

Artur Schnabel

schnell *(Ger.)*   Fast; **schneller**, faster; **nicht schnell**, not fast; **so schnell wie möglich,** as quickly as possible.

Schoenberg, Arnold (1874-1951)   German composer, who lived mainly in Vienna and Berlin until 1933, when Nazi persecution forced him to emigrate to the USA. His early works are in late-Romantic style, but around 1920 he introduced a new method of composition, based on an equal 12-note system, which became known as serial technique, and had a profound effect on other 20th-century composers. His first '12-note' works were the 5 Pieces for piano, Op.23 (1920-3) and the Suite for piano, Op.25. Other piano works: 3 Pieces, Op.11 (1909); 6 Little Pieces, Op.19 (1911), 2 Pieces, Op.33a and b (1928-31); Concerto (1942).

School of Velocity   See **Velocity, School of**.

Schottische *(Ger.)*   'Scottish' A type of ballroom dance similar to the polka, introduced in the mid-19th century. It has no connection with Scotland.

Schubert, Franz (1797-1828)   Austrian composer, one of the great Viennese masters of the late 18th and early 19th centuries. He never held a formal job, and lived all his short life in Vienna, composing over 600 songs among many other works – symphonies, operas, church music, chamber music, and piano music. Schubert was one of the greatest song-writers of all time, while his piano music is rated alongside Haydn's, Mozart's and Beethoven's. Piano works include 21 sonatas, the *Wanderer Fantasy* in C, 1822, 11 Impromptus; *6 Moments musicaux*; *3 Klavierstücke*; Rondo in D; 2 Scherzos; *Hungarian Melody*; 13 Variations in A minor; 48 waltzes; many *Ländler*.

Schubert accompanying a song recital in Vienna

Schumann, Robert (1810-1856)   German composer, pianist and critic. After early training as a pianist, which ended when he injured his hand, he worked as a writer on music in the 1830s. In 1840 he married the pianist Clara Wieck, the immensely talented daughter of his former piano teacher, and began to compose in earnest. His later life, cut short by insanity and disease, was spent as a conductor and teacher in Leipzig, Dresden and Düsseldorf. One of the

An extract from the MS of Schumann's '3 Phantasiestücke' for piano, 1851

Robert and Clara Schumann

greatest Romantic composers, his works include symphonies and other orchestral pieces, chamber music, many songs, and a great deal of important piano music, which is part of the repertory of all pianists today. His Piano Concerto in A minor was written for his wife, as was nearly all his other keyboard music. Piano works include *Abegg Variations* (1830); *Papillons* (1829-31); 12 Concert Studies on Paganini Caprices (2 sets, 1832-3); 6 Intermezzi (1832); 18 *Davidsbündlertänze* (1837); Toccata in C (1830); Allegro in B minor (1831); *Carnaval* (1834-5); 3 sonatas; 8 *Fantasiestücke* (1837); *Études symphoniques* (1834); *Kinderszenen* (1838); *Kreisleriana* (1838); Fantasy in C (1836); *Arabeske* in C (1839); *Blumenstück* (1839); *Faschingsschwank aus Wien* (1839); *3 Romances* (1839); *Album for the Young* (43 pieces in 2 books, 1848); *Waldscenen* (1848-9); *Bunte Blätter* (1852); 3 *Fantasiestücke* (1851); 3 piano sonatas for the young (1853); *Albumblätter* (1832-45); 7 piano pieces in the form of fugues (1853); *5 Gesänge der Frühe* (1853)

Schumann, Clara (née Wieck) (1819-1896)   German pianist, one of the greatest of her time. A child prodigy, she was taught by her father and began touring at an early age. In 1840 she married Robert Schumann and continued her career despite numerous pregnancies. She became the first woman to play Beethoven's *Hammerklavier* Sonata in public and was a lifelong friend of Brahms, who dedicated his 2nd Piano Sonata to her.

schwer *(Ger.)*   Heavy, difficult.

sciolto *(It.)*   Freely, easily.

score   A piece of music which shows all the parts allocated to different performers, i.e. in an orchestral or chamber piece. In a piano quartet, for instance, the pianist will play from the score, which will show him/her not only the piano part, but also the parts of the string players.

Scotch snap   A musical ornament or rhythm, in which a very short note played on the beat is followed by a longer one at a different pitch, occupying the rest of the time-value before the next beat. It is a feature of Scottish folk-music, and was adopted by composers such as Haydn, Beethoven and Mendelssohn.

Scott, Cyril (1879-1970)   English composer and pianist. His short piano pieces in Impressionist styles earned him the title of 'the English Debussy'.

Scriabin   See **Skryabin**.

sec *(Fr.)*   Dry, crisp. An indication used for a note which is to be released immediately after being played, and not allowed to ring on.

Sechzehntel(note) *(Ger.)*   The 16th (note), i.e. the semiquaver.

second
(1) An interval in melody or harmony, either one or 2 steps in the major or minor scale. A major 2nd is a whole tone, e.g. C to D; a minor 2nd is a semitone, i.e. C to D flat or C sharp. An augmented 2nd is 3 semitones, i.e. C to D sharp.
(2) A lower part than the first, e.g. second violin.

second inversion   The position of a 3-note chord in which the 3rd note (the 5th degree) becomes the root. The second inversion of the tonic chord of C major would be G-C-E.

secondo   The lower of the two parts in a piano duet.

second-time bar   See **first- (second-) time bars**

segno *(It.)*   The sign 𝄋 . See **dal segno, al segno**.

segue *(It.)*   A term occurring at the end of a section or movement, indicating that the performer should continue with the next section without a pause. See also **attacca**.

seguidilla (Sp.)   A Spanish dance from Andalusia, in triple time, originally accompanied by castanets and guitar.

sehr *(Ger.)*   Very.

Seiber, Matyás (1905-1960)   Hungarian composer and cellist. He settled first in Germany, and from 1935, in England, where he taught and worked for a publisher. His piano works include the popular *5 Easy Dances* for piano duet.

Seixas, Carlos de (1704-1742)   Portuguese composer, organist and harpsichordist. Worked at the Royal Chapel in Lisbon. He is said to have written over 700 harpsichord pieces or sonatas, of which only 88 survive.

semibreve   The whole-note (**o**), equal to 4 crotchets in length. The **semibreve rest** is written ▬ and is used to indicate a whole bar's rest in any time-signature.

semidemisemiquaver (hemidemisemiquaver)   The 64th note (♬). There are 64 of these in a semibreve.

semiquaver   The 16th note (♪). There are 16 semiquavers in a whole note, or semibreve. The **semiquaver rest** is written like this: ♪ .

semitone   Half a tone. The smallest interval between 2 notes that can be played on a piano.

semplice *(It.)*   Simple, simply.

sempre *(It.)*   Always, still; **sempre più mosso**, getting faster all the time; **sempre piano**, continuing soft.

senza *(It.)*   Without; **senza rall.**, don't get slower. In piano playing, **senza sordini** means 'without dampers', i.e. use the right pedal, which takes the dampers out of action.

septet *(Eng.)*; **septette, septuor** *(Fr.)*; **septetto** *(It.)*; **Septett** *(Ger.)*   Any combination of 7 performers, or a piece of music written for them. Saint-Saëns wrote a septet for piano, trumpet, string quartet and double bass.

septuplet   A group of 7 notes of equal time-values played in the time of 4 or 6.

sequence

(1) The repetition of a passage or phrase at a higher or lower level. Much music, especially from the Baroque and Classical periods is built up through the use of sequences. If the intervals between the notes of the melody are changed at all the sequence is called a **tonal sequence**; if the intervals stay exactly the same, it is called a **real sequence**.

(2) A **chord sequence** is a progression of chords which often lead towards a cadence.

serenade   Originally, a piece of music sung or played in the open air in the evening, often by a lover beneath his girlfriend's window. Later it came to mean a piece of entertainment music for a group of instruments, often for wind instruments alone; but it can be loosely applied for any instrument or voice.

serialism, serial technique   A term applied to a method of composition developed around 1920 by Arnold Schoenberg and his pupils Berg and Webern, in which a series of intervals called a note-row (derived from all 12 notes of the chromatic scale used once in any order determined by the composer), is used to build the melodic and harmonic structure of a piece of music Such music therefore has no key, since all 12 notes are of equal importance. Schoenberg quickly dropped the strictest applications of serial technique, but other composers applied the same principles to rhythmic durations as well as to pitch. Although by the 1960s other innovations had overtaken serial technique, it has had enormous influence on composition in the 20th century.

serioso *(It.)*   Seriously.

Serkin, Rudolf (1903-1991)   Czech pianist. He studied in Vienna, making his début in 1915, and beginning a concert career after the First World War. Settled in the USA. where he became director of the Curtis Institute. Famous for his performances of the classics, but also premiered works by Martin and Prokofiev. Son Peter (b.1947) is now a pianist of international renown.

seventh   An interval encompassing 7 notes of a major or minor scale. E up to D sharp (11 semitones) is a major 7th; E up to D (10 semitones) a minor 7th, and E up to D flat (9 semitones) a diminished 7th. See **intervals**.

Sévérac, Déodat de (1872-1921)   French composer. He was a pupil of d'Indy at the Schola Cantorum in Paris. He wrote operas and symphonic poems, but is now mainly remembered for his short piano pieces, such as *The Musical Box*.

sforzando, sforzato *(It.*, abbreviated *sf* , *sfz*)   'Forcing', 'forced'. The indication that a particular note or passage should be strongly emphasized. Beethoven used the term **sforzato** once – in the first movement of his 'Emperor' Piano Concerto. *sfp* indicates an immediate **piano** after a heavily accented note.

shake   See **trill**.

sharp
    (1) The sign ♯ which, when placed in front of a note, raises it by one semitone. If the key signature has one or more sharps in it, all the appropriate notes in the scale are affected
    (2) To sing or play sharp means that the intonation is pitched too high.

Shostakovich, Dmitri (1906-1975) R u s s i a n
composer and pianist, one of the most important
of the 20th century. In the 1930s his music was
attacked by official critics, and his life was at risk
from Stalin's infamous purges. However, he sur-
vived, and after the war became professor of composition at the Moscow Conservatory. His most
famous works are his symphonies and string quartets, but he also wrote 2 piano concertos and
other piano music, including 2 sonatas; 2 early
sets of preludes; 3 *Fantastic Dances*, 10 *Aphorisms*;
another set of 24 Preludes; a famous set of 24
Preludes and Fugues, Op.87, modelled on Bach,
and dedicated to the Russian pianist Tatiana Nikolaeva; *Children's Notebook*; *7 Dolls' Dances*.

Dmitri Shostakovich

Sibelius, Jean (1865-1957)   Finnish composer.
He studied in Helsinki and at the Vienna Conservatory, and became one of the most important Scan-
dinavian nationalist composers. Best known for
his orchestral and choral music, Sibelius wrote a
quantity of piano music, including 6 Impromptus;
a Sonata; 3 Sonatinas; 10 *Pensées lyriques*; *Lyric
Pieces*; 2 Rondinos; 6 Bagatelles; *5 Romantic
Pieces*; *5 Esquisses*; and 72 pieces published in nine
collections.

siciliano *(It.)*, **sicilienne** *(Fr.)*   'Sicilian'. A dance or piece presumably from
Sicily, often in 6/8 or 12/8 time, and pastoral in character.

sight-reading   The performance of a piece of music at sight, without having
seen it before. The ability to sight-read fluently is essential for any musician,
professional or amateur.

signature   The symbol placed at the beginning of a piece of music, indicating both the key (**key-signature**), and the value of the beat, and the number
of beats to each bar (**time-signature**). A key-signature consists of one of more
sharps or flats (their absence, in tonal music, means that the piece is in C
major or A minor); the time signature looks like a fraction, with the number
of beats in the bar on top, and their value on the bottom. See **time-signature**.

similar motion   See **motion**.

simile, sim. *(It.)*   A shorthand direction used by composers to indicate that
a passage should be played in exactly the same way and with the same
dynamics, etc. as a preceding passage (to save having to write out all the
expression marks).

simple time   The term used to describe time-signatures in which the beats are whole notes rather than dotted notes: 2/4, 3/4, or 4/4.

Sinding, Christian (1856-1941)   Norwegian composer and pianist. He studied in Germany and returned to Oslo, where he spent the rest of his life. He wrote a large number of short piano pieces, including the famous *Rustle of Spring*, one of a collection of 6 Pieces, Op.32.

Six, Les   The name given to a group of French composers, considered avant-garde in their day (around the 1920s). They were: Georges Auric, Louis Durey, Arthur Honegger, Darius Milhaud, Francis Poulenc and Germaine Tailleferre. Honegger, Milhaud and Poulenc were the most important.

sixteenth note   American term for the semiquaver.

sixth   The interval encompassing 6 notes of the major or minor scale. C to A is a major 6th, C to A flat a minor 6th, and C to A sharp an augmented 6th.

sixty-fourth note   The American term for the hemidemisemiquaver.

sketch (*Ger.* **Skizze**, *Fr.* **esquisse**)
(1) A short piece, often for piano. Smetana wrote a set of *Sketches* for piano.
(2) A composer's preliminary jottings, showing how he/she originally conceived a piece of music. Beethoven's sketchbooks are of great interest.

Skryabin, Alexander (1872-1915)   Russian composer and pianist. A child prodigy, he studied at the Moscow Conservatory before spending his life touring as a concert pianist, and occasionally teaching. Piano works: 10 sonatas (no.7 in F sharp is known as the 'White Mass'; no.9 in F as the 'Black Mass'); 24 *Études*; 85 preludes; Concert Allegro in B flat minor, many walzes, impromptus, mazurkas, etc.

Alexander Skryabin

Slavonic Dances   16 dances in popular folk styles by Dvořák, published in 2 sets, as Op.46 (1878) and Op.72 (1886). Originally written for piano duet, but later orchestrated by the composer.

slancio *(It.)*   Dash; **con slancio**, impetuously.

slentando *(It.)*   Becoming slower.

slur   A curved line over or under 2 notes, indicating that the first should be slightly emphasized, and the second lightly lifted off. A curved line covering more than 2 notes is a phrase mark.

Smetana, Bedřich (1824-1884)   Bohemian composer and pianist, one of the most important nationalist composers. After touring Europe as a concert pianist, he became conductor of a choral society in Prague, where several of his operas, including the immensely successful *Bartered Bride*, were produced. In later life he became completely deaf. Best known for his operas and orchestral music, especially the symphonic poem *Ma Vlast* (My country). Piano works include *6 Characteristic Pieces*; *Album Leaves*; *Sketches*; *3 Poetical Polkas*; *Memories of Bohemia*; *Beside the Seashore*; *Dreams*; 14 *Czech Dances*.

Smith, Cyril (1909-1974)   British pianist. After a successful concert career he suffered a thrombosis of the right arm during a Russian tour in 1956. Thereafter he gave three-handed performances with his wife, the pianist Phyllis Sellick, including many premières of works written specially for them. A notable teacher, his pupils included Fanny Waterman and Clifford Benson.

smorzando, smorz. *(It.)*   Dying away, extinguishing the tone.

soave *(It.)*   Gentle, smooth.

soft pedal   The left-hand pedal on the piano, which makes the tone softer either by moving the keyboard so that the hammers strike fewer strings than usual, or by bringing the hammers closer to the strings, so that they strike with less force.

soh, sol   The fifth note of the major scale in tonic sol-fa. In many countries, *sol* means the note G.

solenne, solennemente *(It.)*   Solemn, solemnly.

Soler, Antonio (1729-1783)   Spanish composer and organist. He became a monk in 1752 and entered the monastery of El Escorial the following year. He was much influenced by Domenico Scarlatti, and wrote over 70 fine harpsichord sonatas.

Solfeggietto   A popular piano piece by C.P.E. Bach.

solfeggio *(It.; Fr.* **solfège**)   A method of teaching sight-singing or practising vocal exercises, sometimes called **solmization**, in which the names of the notes are used, e.g. *do, re, mi, fa, so, la ti, do. Do* is always the note C, *re* is D, etc. In France, the term *solfège* means all elementary music teaching. See also **tonic sol-fa**.

solmization   See **tonic sol-fa**.

solo *(It.,* pl. **soli**)   Alone. A piece of music performed by one player, either completely alone, as in a piano piece, or as the soloist in a concerto. Orchestral players may also have to play solo passages.

soloist   The principal performer, e.g. in a concerto.

Solomon (formerly Solomon Cutner) (1902-1988)
British pianist, child prodigy and pupil of Cortot. He
made his début at 8 in Tchaikovsky's 1st Concerto at
the Queen's Hall in London. His brilliant career as
concerto soloist, recitalist and chamber-music player
was cut short by a stroke in his 50s.

Solomon, Yonty (b.1937)   South African pianist.
Studied in London with Myra Hess. Wide-ranging repertoire includes all Charles Ives' piano music, and works
by Sorabji.

sonata (*It.*, from *suonare*, to sound; *Fr.* **sonate**, *Ger.*,
Sonate)   A piece for piano, or for another instrument,
e.g. violin, flute, cello, with piano accompaniment, usually in several movements. Originally, it meant any
music which was played rather than sung. In the Baroque era, two types of sonata developed, the **sonata
da chiesa** (church sonata), a serious piece usually in
four movements (slow-fast-slow-fast), and the **sonata
da camera** (chamber sonata), originally a sequence of

Solomon

dance movements, suitable for entertainment. Both
types were usually scored for 2 or 3 string players with keyboard accompaniment. Some of the earliest keyboard sonatas were written by Bach's predecessor Johann Kuhnau (1660-1722), and these were developed by Domenico
Scarlatti in Italy and by C.P.E. Bach in Germany. Haydn, Mozart and
Beethoven developed the Classical **piano sonata** – by now usually in 3
movements (fast-slow-fast) to its highest level: Beethoven's 32 examples,
including the famous *Moonlight*, *Appassionata*, *Pathétique* and *Hammerklavier*
sonatas, are considered to be the peaks of the repertory.

The first movement of a Classical sonata is usually in sonata form; the
slow movement is usually lyrical, while the last may be a set of variations or
a rondo. Beethoven sometimes introduced a 3rd movement between slow
movement and finale, at first a minuet, and later a scherzo, as in his symphonies. Most Romantic composers, including Schubert, Schumann, Brahms and
Liszt, wrote piano sonatas (Liszt's great B minor Sonata is in a single huge
movement). In the 20th century, composers up to Boulez and Tippett have
continued to write sonatas for piano.

sonata form   A musical form often used for the first movement of a sonata,
concerto or symphony from the Classical period onwards. The basic type has
three sections: the exposition, in which 2 themes (or subjects) – in contrasting keys – are presented, and often repeated; a development, in which the
material from the exposition is worked out further in free style through
various keys; and a recapitulation, in which the exposition is repeated with
slight differences but ends in its original key with a coda.

sonata rondo   A combination of sonata and rondo form, often used for the finales of sonatas and symphonies from Mozart and Beethoven onwards.

sonatina *(It.)*; **sonatine** *(Fr.)*   A little sonata. A short sonata, originally often composed (e.g. by Haydn, Mozart and Beethoven) for teaching purposes. Later sonatinas, including those by Ravel Busoni, and Ireland, can be very difficult.

Songs without Words   See **Lieder ohne Wörte**.

sonore *(Fr.)*, **sonoro** *(It.)*   Sonorous, with full tone.

sopra *(It.)*   On, above; **come di sopra**, as above. Occasionally used in piano music to indicate that one hand crosses over the other.

soprano   The highest female voice, or a high instrumental register.

sordino, sordina, sord. *(It.,* pl. **sordini)**   Mute. On the piano, it means dampers; **senza sordini**, without dampers, means 'put the sustaining pedal down'.

sospirando, sospirante *(It.)*   Plaintive, as if sighing.

An early 18th-century spinet by Thomas Hitchcock

sostenuto *(It.)*   Sustained. Hold each note in a passage to its full value, creating a smooth flow. The term may also imply a slightly slower tempo.

sotto voce *(It.)*   'Below the voice'. Quietly, in an undertone.

sound-board
(1) The wooden board on a keyboard instrument placed behind or under the strings, to amplify the sound.
(2) The upper part of the wind chest on an organ, on which the pipes sound.

sourdine *(Fr.)*   Mute; **en sourdine**, muted; **mettez (ôtez) les sourdines**, put on (take off) mutes.

Spiel, spielen *(Ger.)*   Play; to play.

spinet *(Fr.* **épinette**; *It.* **spinetta**).   A small early keyboard instrument dating originally from the late 15th century, suitable for use in the home. The strings ran diagonally in front of the player, or even parallel to the keyboard. They were plucked by plectra, as on the harpsichord, and the usual compass was 4 octaves.

spirito, spiritoso *(It.)* Spirit; with spirit.

spiritual Religious folksongs of the American negroes of the Deep South, especially sung by slaves working on 19th-century cotton plantations. Dvořák used the spiritual *Swing low, sweet chariot* in his *New World* Symphony, Gershwin used spirituals in his opera *Porgy and Bess*, and Tippett in his oratorio *A Child of our Time*.

square piano An early type of piano, made from about 1740 up to the mid-19th century, in which the mechanism was enclosed in a horizontal rectangular box. See **piano** (2).

An early 19th-century square piano

staccato *(It.)* Short, detached. A way of playing a note or sequence of notes so that it is immediately released, creating a short, sharp sound. Staccato is indicated by a dot under or over the note: a small dagger-point instead of a dot indicates **staccatissimo** – very short and detached.

staff, stave The system of 5 parallel lines on which most Western music is written. The pitch is determined by the clef placed at the beginning of each staff.

stark *(Ger.)* Strong.

Steinway and Sons American firm of piano manufacturers founded in 1853 in New York. Having invented the iron-framed piano in 1855, Steinway began making world-famous concert grands in the 1860s. Steinway pianos are still favoured by many top artists.

stem The tail attached to a note-head in musical notation.

stesso See **istesso**.

Still *(Ger.)* Peaceful.

Stockhausen, Karlheinz (b.1928) German composer, a pupil of Messaien, and one of the pioneers of electronic music.

A modern Steinway grand piano

Since 1971 he has taught composition at the Cologne Music High-School. Piano works include a series of 11 *Klavierstücke*, written in the 1950s, which explore various aspects of avant-garde keyboard techniques.

stop

(1) The row of pipes on the organ, operated by handles (or now electronically). Both pipes and handles are called stops. The stops can change the sound emitted by the pipes. See **organ**.

(2) A similar system to the above, on the harpsichord, designed to vary the tone-colour, e.g. to sound like a lute.

straccinato *(It.)*   Stretched out, the same as **ritardando**.

strathspey   A traditional Scottish dance in 4/4 time, noted for its dotted rhythms.

Strauss, Richard (1864-1949)   German composer, particularly noted for his operas and his orchestral music. His early Piano Sonata in B minor dates from 1881, and he wrote several works for piano and orchestra, including the *Burleske* in D minor.

Stravinsky, Igor (1882-1971)   Russian composer, a pupil of Rimsky-Korsakov. Left Russia during the Revolution, and settled first in Paris, and then in the USA. One of the most important 20th-century composers, Stravinsky is particularly famous for his ballets, including *The Rite of Spring*, *The Firebird* and *Petrushka*, his orchestral music, and his opera *The Rake's Progress*. Piano works include a Concerto for piano and wind instruments (1923-4); *Capriccio* for piano and orchestra (1928-9); *Movements* for piano and orchestra (1958-9); Sonata in F sharp minor (1903-4); 4 Studies; *3 Easy Pieces* for piano duet; 5 *Easy Pieces* for piano duet; *Piano Rag-Music*; Sonata (1924), *Serenade in A*; Concerto for 2 solo pianos, *Tango*; *Circus Polka*; Sonata for 2 pianos (1943-4), and a piano arrangement of 3 movements from *Petrushka*.

strepitoso *(It.)*   Noisy.

stretto *(It.)*   Drawn together.

(1) Faster tempo.

(2) In a fugue, a passage when all the 'voices' enter quickly, overlapping with each other. Such a passage often occurs towards the end, as a climax to the whole piece.

stringendo *(It.)*   'Squeezing'. Increase the speed, to heighten the intensity of the music.

strings   The thin pieces of gut or wire which produce the sound on a stringed instrument, such as the violin, and on keyboard instruments such as the piano (by being hit with hammers), or on the harpsichord, spinet or virginals, by being plucked.

strophic   The term given to a musical form in which a section – such as the verse of a song – is repeated several times using the same music. The opposite is **through-composed**.

Stück *(Ger.)*   Piece.

study   See **étude**.

subdominant   The 4th note of the major or minor scale.

subito, sub. *(It.)*   Suddenly, immediately; *p* **sub.**, suddenly soft; **attacca subito**, go on immediately to the next section or movement without a break; **volti subito (V.S.)**. turn over the page quickly.

subject   The term used to describe a motif, phrase or tune which forms part of the principal musical material of a larger piece. In sonata form, there is usually a principal (first) subject in the tonic key, and a contrasting second subject, often in the dominant key. In fugue, the subject is the main tune which is stated at the beginning, and then by all the parts (or 'voices') in turn.

submediant   The sixth note of the major or minor scale.

suite *(Fr.* **ordre**, *Ger.* **Partien**, *It.* **partita**)   Originally a sequence of move-ments for instrumental ensemble, usually in dance styles. During the Baroque era, the suite became more standardized, to include four basic dances: allemande, courante, sarabande and gigue, with other dances such as minuet, gavotte, bourrée, passepied or rigaudon added as the composer wished. Nearly all the movements were in the same key, and in simple binary form. Bach's French and English suites for solo keyboard are particularly impor-tant, as are Handel's 16 harpsichord suites. French composers such as Couperin and Rameau gave the pieces in their suites fanciful titles.

Suite bergamasque (Bergomask Suite)   A suite of four pieces by Debussy, completed 1905, in imitation of old styles and comprising *Prélude, Menuet, Clair de lune* and *Passepied*.

suivez *(Fr.)*   Follow.
    (1) Begin the next section or movement without a break (see **attacca**).
    (2) Direction to an accompanist to follow any changes in speed made by the soloist.

supertonic   The second note of the major or minor scale.

suspension   The harmonic device whereby one note in a chord is held over while the harmony changes, producing a momentary discord, which is then resolved by the held note dropping by one step to a note in the new chord. Suspensions were much used in Baroque music to create a sense of tension.

sustaining pedal   See **pedal** (1) and (2).

sussurando, susurrante *(It.)*   Whispering.

syncopation   A rhythmic device used to disrupt a regular rhythmic beat, e.g. by accenting a weak instead of a strong beat, by holding beats over or by putting rests on strong beats. Syncopation is an essential ingredient of all pop music from ragtime and jazz onwards.

synthesizer   An electronic device for producing and mixing sounds, usually controlled from a keyboard. Synthesizers can imitate any musical sound, from a solo piano to a full orchestra.

system   The term used to describe a group of staves. In piano music, a system will consist of 2 staves, bracketed together (for right and left hands). In an orchestral score, a system will comprise as many staves as are needed to accommodate the instrumental parts for a particular piece.

Szymanowski, Karol (1882-1937)   Polish composer, who worked in Russia and Poland. Director of the Warsaw Conservatory 1926-30; one of the important 20th-century nationalists. Piano works include *Symphonie concertante* for piano and orchestra (1931-2); 3 sonatas; 9 Preludes (1900); Variations in B flat minor (1901); 4 Studies (1902); *Variations on a Polish Folk-theme* (1904); Fantasy in F minor (1905); *Métopes* (3 poems, 1915); 3 *Masks* (1916); 20 Mazurkas (1924-6); *4 Polish Dances* (1926); 2 Mazurkas (1934)

T

tacet *(Lat.)*   The indication for a silence lasting quite a long time, usually found in orchestral parts.

tango   An Argentinian dance, which became popular in ballrooms in the USA and Europe around the time of the First World War. It is danced by a couple at a slow walking pace, and has a characteristic dotted rhythm.

tanto *(It.)*   So much; **allegro non tanto**, fast but not too fast.

Tanz *(Ger.,* pl. **Tanze)**   Dance.

tarantella *(It.)*   A lively Neapolitan dance in 6/8 time, which may take its name either from the town of Taranto, in southern Italy, or from the spider called the tarantula. It was once believed that the spider's bite caused a disease called tarantism, which could only be cured by dancing very fast. The tarantella is in quick, continuous quavers, and was popular with 19th-century composers such as Rossini, Liszt and Mendelssohn.

tasto *(It.)*
  (1) The fingerboard of a stringed instrument.
  (2) The keys of a keyboard instrument. In figured bass playing (see **basso continuo**), **tasto solo** means play the written bass notes only, without adding chords above.

Tausig, Carl (1841-1871)   Polish pianist, one of the most formidable virtuosi of his day. He studied with Liszt and became a friend of Brahms. He settled in Berlin, where he founded an academy for highly gifted pupils. Died of typhoid fever. His transcriptions of works by Bach, Schubert and Weber are still performed today.

Tchaikovsky, Pyotr Ilyich (1840-1893)
Russian composer. He began his career as a professor of harmony at the newly-opened Moscow Conservatory. Around 1877 he was befriended by a widowed millionairess, Madame von Meck, who supported him financially so that he could compose full-time. Best known for his 6 symphonies and other orchestral music,

Pyotr Ilyich Tchaikovsky

his ballets (*Swan Lake*, *Sleeping Beauty*, *The Nutcracker*) and his operas. Piano music includes 2 concertos (no.1 in B flat minor is the famous one), *Valse Caprice*; *Capriccio*; 3 Pieces, Op.9, *Nocturne and Humoresque*, Op.10; *6 Pieces on One Theme*, Op.21; Sonata in G; *The Seasons* (12 pieces); *Children's Album*; 60 more pieces, published in 4 collections, Opp. 39, 40, 51 and 72; *Dumka*, Op.59.

Telemann, Georg Philipp (1681-1767)   German composer and organist, considered in his lifetime one of Germany's greatest composers. He wrote perhaps more music, of all types, than any other composer ever, including 40 operas, more than 40 Passion settings, and 600 instrumental overtures. He also wrote a quantity of keyboard music for harpsichord and organ.

temperament   The fine tuning of intervals so that there is no audible difference between, e.g. the notes D sharp and E flat. On a piano keyboard, these notes are played by the same key, but players of stringed instruments would make a minute difference between them, so that D sharp played on a violin against E flat on a piano would sound very slightly 'out of tune'. Equal temperament, in which all semitones are equal, and which is used for pianos, organs and other instruments of fixed pitch, was finally introduced in the mid-19th century. Before then, it was impossible to play in certain keys.

tempo (*It.*, pl. **tempi**)   The speed at which a piece of music is played;
a tempo, resume the original speed (after some slowing down or speeding up); **tempo primo**, at the original speed; **tempo comodo**, at a safe and comfortable speed. See also **giusto**.

temps (*Fr.*)
    (1) See **tempo**.
    (2) Beat.

ten.   Abbreviation for **tenuto**.

tenebroso (*It.*)   Gloomy.

tenendo (*It.*)   Sustaining.

tenero, teneramente (*It.*)   Tender; tenderly.

tenor
    (1) A high male voice.
    (2) Instruments of a similar range to the tenor voice, e.g. tenor saxophone.
    (3) The viola.

tenor clef   See **clef**.

tenth   The interval of an octave and a 3rd.

tenuto (*It.*)   Held. Hold a note for its full value, or even longer; **ben tenuto**, very much held on.

ternary   In 3 parts. A piece in ternary form is in 3 sections, of which the first and last are the same or very similar, and the middle section is different (ABA).

tessitura *(It.)*   Texture. The term is applied to describe the relative positions of certain musical parts, e.g. high, medium or low.

tetrachord   An old scale, no longer used, based on 4 notes. A major scale is made up of 2 consecutive tetrachords.

Thalberg, Sigismond (1812-1871)   Austrian pianist and composer, born in Switzerland. He made many concert tours of Europe, playing many times in London. One of the greatest virtuosi of his day, he was the only serious rival to Liszt, and in later life was known as 'Old Arpeggio'. Wrote numerous piano pieces, and contributed to the **Hexameron** (1837).

Sigismond Thalberg

theme   A group of successive notes which form a recognizable tune, which can then be used as the basis for the construction of a piece of music. Many composers have written sets of variations on a theme - either composed by themselves or others, or a well known tune. Musicals and films often have a theme-song (e.g. *Memory*, from *Cats*), which recurs throughout at important points.

third   An interval encompassing 3 notes of a major or minor scale. In the scale of C major, the interval C to E is a major 3rd; C to E flat is a minor 3rd; and C sharp to E flat is a diminished 3rd.

third inversion   The position of a 4-note chord in which the 4th note has become the root, or lowest note. For instance, the chord A-C sharp-E-G in fourth position would be G-A-C sharp -E, or G-C sharp-E-A.

root position   3rd inversions

thirty-second-note   American term for the **demisemiquaver**.

thorough bass   See **basso continuo**.

through-composed (*Ger.* **durchkomponiert**)   A term used to decribe a composition which runs straight through, without any repeated section. The opposite is **strophic**, in which a section, such as the verse of a song, is repeated musically.

tie (or **bind**)   A curved line placed between 2 notes of the same pitch, to indicate that the second note is tied to the first, i.e. that they should be performed as one note, with their time-values added together.

tief *(Ger.)*   Deep.

tierce de Picardie *(Fr.)*   Picardy 3rd. The name given to the last chord in a piece of music in a minor key, if that final chord has an unexpected major 3rd in it. It was mainly used in music of the Renaissance and Baroque eras.

timbre *(Fr.)*   Tone-colour. The particular sound of a voice or instrument.

time   The basic pulse of a piece of music, e.g. 3/4 time = 3 crotchet beats to the bar.

time-signature   The symbol, looking like a fraction, placed at the beginning of a piece of music to indicate how many beats there are in each bar (the upper figure), and the value of each beat expressed in terms of its relation to a semibreve (the lower figure). A time-signature of $\frac{4}{4}$ would mean each bar contained 4 crotchet beats. Time-signatures can vary from bar to bar, especially in more modern music.

Tippett, (Sir) **Michael** (b.1905)   English composer. He began studying music at 18, and later became Director of Music at Morley College in London. From 1951 onwards he has devoted his time to composition. Best-known for his operas (*A Midsummer Marriage, King Priam, The Knot Garden, The Ice Break, New Year*) and his wartime oratorio *A Child of Our Time*, he has also written 4 important piano sonatas.

toccata *(It.)*   'Touched'. An early keyboard piece, originally like a short prelude, usually in flowing note-values, which could show off the player's touch. Later, the toccata was often paired with a fugue or *ricercare*. Bach wrote both toccatas and fugues, and some toccatas for harpsichord in several movements.

tombeau *(Fr.)*   Tomb. A memorial work, for a recently-dead friend or colleague. The term was much used in 17th and 18th-century French music; and has been revived this century, e.g. in Ravel's *Le tombeau de Couperin*.

ton *(Fr.)*, **Ton** *(Ger.)*   Pitch, key, note, tone, sound.

tonal   Based on the system of keys. Tonal music is the opposite of atonal, i.e., it has a key centre.

tonality   Key. A piece can be in the tonality of C (in the key of C). **Bitonality**, the use of 2 different keys at the same time. **Polytonality**, the use of several different keys at once. **Atonality**, in no specific key.

tone
    (1) A musical sound.
    (2) The interval of a major second.
    (3) The American term for **note**.
    (4) The quality of sound produced by a player or instrument, e.g. harsh tone, sweet tone.

tone-colour   The same as **timbre**.

tonic   The basic key-note of a scale or key – the first note of that scale. The tonic of C major is the note C; the tonic of D minor is the note D, etc.

tonic sol-fa (solmization)   An English sight-singing and notational system first developed in the 1830s and popularized by John Curwen (1816-80). It is based on the so-called 'movable-*doh*' system – i.e. the note *doh* can be applied to the tonic note of any key. The notes of the major scale are called (in the English system) by the names *doh*, *ray*, *me*, *fah*, *soh*, *lah*, *te*, *doh*; and are written *d*, *r*, *m*, *f*, *s*, *l*, *t*, *d*. For sharpened notes, the vowel is changed to 'e', so *doh* (if sharp) would be *de*. For flattened notes, the vowel is changed to *a*, so *soh* flattened would be *sa*. See also **solfeggio**.

toujours *(Fr.)*   Always, still; **toujours lent**, slow always.

touch   The weight required to press down the keys of a keyboard instrument. A player's 'touch' is assessed according to how he or she controls the pressure of fingers, hands and arm to produce the required sound, and is one of the most important aspects of piano playing.

traîné *(Fr.)*   Dragged.

tranquillo *(It.)*   Quietly, calmly.

Transcendental Studies (Études d'exécution transcendente)
    (1) A set of 12 virtuoso piano studies by Liszt, published in 1852. Their titles are: 1. *Preludio*; 2. [in A minor]; 3. *Paysage*; 4. *Mazeppa*; 5. *Feux follets*; 6. *Vision*; 7. *Eroica*; 8. *Wilde Jagd*; 9. *Ricordanza*; 10. [in F minor]; 11. *Harmonies du soir*; 12. *Chasse-neige*
    (2) **Transcendental Studies after Paganini (Études d'exécution transcendante d'après Paganini)** Liszt's set of 6 monumental piano studies based on themes by Paganini, published in 1840. No.3 is *La campanella*; no.5 is *La chasse*. In 1851 Liszt revised them under the title *Grandes études de Paganini*.

transcription

(1) An arrangement of a piece of music for something other than its original scoring. Many orchestral pieces have been transcribed for piano solo or duet.

(2) The conversion of a piece from one type of notation to another, especially with very old music, where notation and time-values are written differently, and have to be 'transcribed' into modern notation.

transition

(1) A link passage between one section of a piece and the next.

(2) Modulation from one key to another.

transposing instruments   Instruments in which the sound produced is at a different pitch from the notated music. It applies to some woodwind and brass instruments, which are built in certain keys to avoid difficulties when playing in flat or sharp keys.

transposition   Altering the pitch of a piece, but not its intervals or anything else. A piece can be transposed into any other key: it will sound the same, but at a different pitch.

Trauermusik *(Ger.)*   Funeral, or mourning music.

treble

(1) The highest voice in a choir, usually applied to children's voices.

(2) The top part of a composition.

(3) Instruments with similar pitch to the treble voice, such as the treble recorder.

treble clef   See **clef**.

tre corde *(It.)*   3 strings. The direction used in piano playing to cancel the instruction to use the soft pedal (*una corda*).

tremolo *(It.)*   Shaking, trembling. In piano music, a **tremolo** is indicated:

which means that the 2 notes should be alternated as quickly as possible, giving an effect like a trill.

trepak   A fast Russian dance in 2/4 time.

très *(Fr.)*   Very; e.g. **très vite**, very fast.

triad   A chord containing 3 notes – tonic, 3rd and 5th, e.g. C-E-G in the key of C major. An augmented triad will have a sharpened 5th; a diminished triad will contain a diminished 5th.

trill (or **shake**)   A musical ornament, often indicated *tr* , in which 2 adjacent

cent notes are alternated very quickly. In Baroque and Classical music, trills normally begin on the upper of the 2 notes, which should be played on the beat; in later music, trills usually begin on the lower note. Trills are often found just before a cadence, and often occur on the supertonic before it finally drops to the tonic. The cadenzas of Baroque and Classical concertos often end with a trill (or series of trills on different notes), indicating that the orchestra should prepare for re-entry.

trio

(1) A group of 3 performers, or a piece of music written for them. A piano trio usually consists of piano, violin and cello. A trio (the music) often has 3 movements, e.g. Schubert's Piano Trios in B flat and E flat.

(2) The middle section of a minuet, march or scherzo, usually slower in speed and more rustic in style. Originally, trios were played by 3 instruments.

trio sonata A Baroque composition in several movements for 2 upper instruments (usually violins), cello and keyboard continuo (4 performers in all - which often causes confusion). A solo sonata in the Baroque era meant a similar piece for one upper instrument with cello and keyboard continuo (3 performers in all).

triple concerto A concerto for 3 solo performers. Beethoven's Triple Concerto is scored for piano, violin and cello with orchestra.

triple time Music which is divided into groups of 3 beats, e.g. 3/4, 3/8, 9/8.

triplet A group of three notes of equal time-value, played in the time of 2. Usually indicated by a small figure 3 placed over the group.

tritone The interval of the augmented 4th, consisting of 3 whole tones, e.g. C to F sharp. In early (medieval) music, the interval was considered to sound so ugly that it was called the 'devil in music', and avoided like the plague.

troppo *(It.)* Too much; **allegro ma non troppo**, fast, but not too fast.

'Trout' Quintet A composition for violin, viola, cello, double bass and piano by Schubert, written in 1819. It is so nicknamed because the 4th of its 5 movements is a set of variations on Schubert's own song *The Trout*.

trumpet tune, trumpet voluntary A Baroque piece, usually for harpsichord or organ, which imitates the sound of the trumpet. The famous *Trumpet Voluntary* once thought to be by Purcell is actually not by him at all, but by his contemporary Jeremiah Clarke.

tune

(1) Another name for melody.

(2) 'To tune' means to adjust an instrument so that it sounds 'in tune', i.e. the intonation is correct.

tuning fork   A metal instrument with 2 prongs, invented in 1711, which when struck so that it vibrates, produces a pure sound against which instruments and voices can check their own pitch. In orchestras, a tuning-fork which gives the note A is used.

turca, alla *(It.)*   See **alla turca**.

turn *(It.* **gruppetto***)*   An ornament consisting of 4 notes: the note above, the note itself, the note below, and the note itself again. It is indicated by this sign:

A turn may be played either instead of the note iself, or after it, depending on where the sign is placed, and the speed at which it is performed varies according to the speed of the music, but is normally quite fast. Sometimes the upper or lower note in the turn needs to be sharpened, flattened, or naturalized, which is indicated thus:

The inverted turn, usually indicated like this:

begins on the lower, rather than the upper note.

tutto, tutti *(It.)*   All. The *tutti* passages in a concerto are where everybody plays, but not the soloist; **tutte le corde**, in piano music, is a direction used to cancel the instruction *una corda* (play with the soft pedal down).

twelve-note, twelve-tone   See **serialism**.

tyrolienne *(Fr.)*   In the style of a dance from the Austrian Tyrol.

tzigane *(Fr.)*   Gypsy. Also the title of a piano and violin duo by Ravel.

U

Übung *(Ger.)*   Exercise.

Uchida, Mitsuko (b. 1948)   Japanese pianist. Studied in Tokyo and with Wilhelm Kempff in Vienna, where she made her début. Prizewinner in several major competitions, including Beethoven (1969), International Chopin (1970) and Leeds (1975). Regarded as a fine interpreter of Mozart, Beethoven, Chopin, Schumann and Debussy.

Mitsuko Uchida

una corda *(It.)*   One string. Use the soft pedal (which causes the hammers to strike one string only, producing a softer tone).

und *(Ger.)*   And.

ungherese *(It.)*   Hungarian.

unison   Together, i.e. all voices or parts simultaneously singing/playing the same note or notes.

up-beat
(1) The beat before a bar line which may begin a piece (see **anacrusis**).
(2) The upward movement (in tempo) of a hand or baton by which a conductor indicates that a piece is about to start, and the speed at which it should be played.

upright piano   See **piano**.

V

V.S.   Abbreviation of **volti subito**, turn the page over quickly.

valse *(Fr.)* Waltz; **valsetto** *(It.)*   little waltz.

Valses nobles et sentimentales (Noble and sentimental waltzes)   A composition for piano by Ravel (1911), later orchestrated.

vamp, vamping   The improvised piano accompaniment to a song or instrumental piece, often done by a pianist who can only play by ear.

variation   The varied version of a theme or tune, often with added decorations, or in which the tune is turned upside down, heard with altered note-values, or treated in various other ways. Many composers have written sets of piano variations on a theme, e.g. Mozart's variations on *Ah, vous dirai-je, maman* (the same tune as *Twinkle, twinkle, little star*), and Beethoven's *Diabelli Variations*. Rakhmaninov's *Rhapsody on a theme of Paganini* for piano and orchestra, based on the 24th Caprice, is perhaps the most famous set of its kind.

veloce, velocemente *(It.)*   Very fast indeed.

Velocity, School of   A famous set of piano exercises and studies by Czerny, Op.299.

Versetzung *(Ger.)*   Transposition.

via *(It.)*   Away; **via sordini**, take the mutes off.

Viennese School   A general term given to the composers active in Vienna in the late 18th and early 19th centuries, especially Haydn, Mozart, Beethoven and Schubert. A similar group, Schoenberg, Webern and Berg, active in the first decades of the 20th century, are sometimes referred to as the **Second Viennese School**.

vif *(Fr.)*   Lively.

vigoroso *(It.)*   Vigorously.

Vingt regards sur l'enfant Jésus (20 glances at the infant Jesus)
A sequence of piano pieces (1944) by Olivier Messiaen, celebrating the birth of the Saviour in rapt, ecstatic musical language.

virginals   A name first used around 1460 to describe keyboard instruments in which the strings were plucked. During the Elizabethan period, the virgin-

A virginal by Giovanni Celestini, Venice 1593

A double virginal by Jan Ruckers, 1623

als became particularltly popular in England. A typical instrument was shaped like an oblong box on legs, with one set of strings lying parallel to the keyboard. Double virginals had 2 keyboards, one placed above or beside the other. English composers such as Byrd, Bull, Farnaby and Gibbons all wrote music for virginals, much of which is contained in the *Fitzwilliam Virginal Book*.

virtuoso *(It.)* A performer or performance of great skill or technical accomplishment.

Visions de l'Amen   A suite in 7 movements for 2 pianos (1943) by Olivier Messaien.

Visions fugitives   20 piano pieces by Prokofiev, Op.22, composed between 1915 and 1917.

vite *(Fr.)*   Quick.

vivace *(It.)*   Fast and lively; **vivacissimo**, very fast.

vivo *(It.)*   Lively.

voce, voci *(It.)*   Voice, voices; **colla voce**, 'with the voice'; – a direction to a piano accompanist to follow the singer's variations of tempo closely.

voice   In keyboard music, one particular strand or line of music in harmony or counterpoint, also known as a 'part'. A fugue, even when played on an instrument, is described as having several voices.

volante *(It.)*   'Flying'. Fast, light.

volta *(It.)*
    (1) Time; **prima volta**, first time.
    (2) A quick dance of the Elizabethan period, in triple time. also known as **lavolta**.

volti subito *(It., abbreviated* **V.S.***)*   Turn the page over quickly.

voluntary
    (1) A term applied to an improvised composition in the 16th century.
    (2) A solo for organ, played at the beginning or end of an Anglican church service, usually while the congregation assembles and departs.

vuota, vuoto *(It.)*   'Empty'. A general pause, i.e. a bar in which all instruments are resting.

W

W. The German abbreviation for **Werk** (pl. **Werke**), work(s), i.e. the same as Opus. BWV stands for *Bach Werke-Verzeichnis* (Index to Bach's works); WoO stands for *Werke ohne Opuszahl* (Work without opus number).

'Waldstein' Sonata   The nickname given to Beethoven's Piano Sonata in C major, Op.53 (1804). dedicated to his friend and patron Count Waldstein.

Waldscenen   (Woodland scenes) 9 pieces for piano by Robert Schumann, Op.82 (1848-9).

Waltz (*Ger.* **Waltzer**, *Fr.* **valse**)   A dance of German origin in 3/4 time which became very popular as a ballroom dance in the last quarter of the 18th century. Many people were shocked when it was first introduced, mainly because the dancing couples held each other closely. Beethoven, Schubert and Brahms all wrote piano waltzes, and Beethoven's famous 'Diabelli Variations' are based on a waltz theme, as is Weber's piano rondo *Introduction to the Dance* – but the most famous examples of the later Viennese waltz are those for orchestra by Johann Strauss I. Chopin first experienced the waltz in Vienna, and later followed Weber's example, producing 14 waltzes ranging in mood from brilliant virtuosity to poignant sadness, which are regarded as the finest examples for solo piano.

'Wanderer' Fantasy   The nickname given to Schubert's Fantasia in C major for piano, 1822. The slow section is based on a theme taken from his song *The Wanderer* (1816). Liszt later made an arrangement of the work for piano and orchestra.

Weber, Carl Maria von (1786-1826)   German composer, conductor and pianist, a pupil of Michael Haydn. Worked at various German courts, and as director of the Prague Opera, before becoming court kapellmeister at Dresden (1817), where he wrote his famous opera *Der Freischütz*. Died in London of tuberculosis. Piano works include 2 concertos (C, 1810; E flat, 1812); *Konzertstück* in F minor for piano and orchestra (1821); 4 sonatas; 4 sets of variations; 12 Allemandes; Ecossaises; *Grande Polonaise*; *Rondo brillante*; *Polacca brillante*; and *Aufförderung zum Tanz* (Invitation to the dance), 1819.

Carl Maria von Weber

Webern, Anton (1883-1945)   Austrian composer and conductor, a pupil of Schoenberg 1904-8. Conductor and musical adviser to Austrian Radio 1927-38; an advocate of atonality, and then of strict serial technique. His music was banned by the Nazis. After the war had ended, he was accidentally shot by an American soldier. Webern's music – some of which only lasts a few bars – had enormous influence on later composers, especially Boulez and Stockhausen. Piano works: *Stück*, 1924; Variations, Op.27, 1936.

'Wedge' Fugue   The nickname given to Bach's organ fugue in E minor, written some time between 1727 and 1736. It is so called because the subject develops in ever-increasing intervals, so that it is shaped like a wedge.

Wenig *(Ger.)*   Little; **ein wenig langsamer**, a little slower.

whole note   American term for the semibreve.

whole tone   The interval of 2 semitones, e.g. from C up to D. A **whole-tone scale** consists only of intervals of a whole tone, with no semitones. Only 2 different versions of this scale are possible on the piano, one starting a semitone above the other. Debussy used the whole-tone scale in his compositions, to loosen up the harmony and create a fluid effect.

Wiegenlied *(Ger.)*   A cradle song, or lullaby.

'Winter Wind' Study   The nickname given to Chopin's *Étude* in A minor, Op.25 no.11.

Wittgenstein, Paul (1887-1961)   Austrian pianist. A pupil of Leschetitzky, he lost his right arm during World War I. Thereafter he specialized in music for left hand, much written for him, e.g. by Ravel (Concerto), Prokofiev (4th Concerto), Richard Strauss (*Parergon zum Symphonia Domestica*).

Wöhltemperierte Klavier, Das   (The Well-Tempered Clavier). The title given by Bach to 2 sets of 24 preludes and fugues for keyboard in all the major and minor keys, intended to demonstrate the advantages of equal temperament. The first set was written in 1722 and the second in 1744. The whole set is also known as 'The 48'.

Y

Yamaha   Japanese firm of instrument manufacturers, now making fine upright pianos and concert grands, as well as digital and electronic instruments.

A modern Yamaha 6' grand piano

Z

zart *(Ger.)*   Tender, soft.

ziemlich *(Ger.)*   Rather,   moderately.

zigeuner *(Ger.)*   Gypsy.

Zimerman, Krystian (b.1956)
Polish pianist. Won 1st prize at 1975 International Chopin Competition, making his London debut 2 years later. Greatly respected as a supreme exponent of Chopin.

Krystian Zimerman

zingaresca, alla *(It.)*   In gypsy style.

zu 2 *(Ger.)*   Divide into 2 parts.

zweimal *(Ger.)*   Twice.